LOUVRE

Pocket Guide

The Louvre, eight hundred years of history

The Louvre, its four hundred three rooms and tens of thousands of works dating back to 8000 BC, is now a museum filled with a very long history, which started eight hundred years ago...

In the origins: a fortress

The Louvre, a fortress erected at the initiative of Philip Augustus, was originally destined to strengthen the compound built in 1190 to secure Paris, capital of the kingdom of France. The castle, built on the "Lupara" site from which its name derives, was therefore a first-line defensive building, around which a suburb gradually grew, before becoming the home of French kings. In 1356, the Hundred Years' War pushed to the construction by Étienne Marcel of a new wall enclosing the right bank neighborhoods, integrating the Louvre into the city. The castle thus became under Charles V a royal residence, furnished and embellished by the architect Raymond du Temple, before being disinvested for a whole century.

The Louvre gained the grandness of a royal palace when King Francis I decided to settle there in 1528. The king, a builder and a patron of the arts, had major works undertaken under the aegis of Pierre Lescot, who imagined, to replace the medieval west wing, a Renaissance-style building decorated by Jean Goujon. Henry II continued the work, ordering the layout, on the ground floor, of the ceremonial hall of the Caryatids where he organized parties and celebrations. His widow, Catherine de Medici, commissioned the building of the Tuileries, further west, from plans drawn up by Philibert Delorme and completed by Jean Bullant. But the work was never completed. During the 17th century, the architectural plans from the Renaissance kept being followed, albeit redesigned to a monumental scale. As early as Henri IV's reign, the decision was made to bring together the Louvre and Tuileries castles with a 1.5km long gallery, built along the Seine from 1595 to 1609. Under Louis XIII's reign, the Cour Carrée's surface was multiplied by four, with the construction, by Jacques Lemercier, of the Pavillon de l'Horloge. This large square surface was only completed under Louis XIV's

The former Hall of Henri IV's Antiques.
☞ Department of Greek, Etruscan and Roman Antiquities, Denon wing, ground floor, room 27

reign after ample controversy. An international competition, won by the famous Italian artist Bernini, was held to design the east wing of the Cour Carrée, to be used as the palace's entrance. Nevertheless, the building was completed to according to a French project by Louis Le Vau, Charles Le Brun and Claude Perrault, a plan which gave us the famous Colonnade du Louvre. Beside this great endeavor, many embellishment works were undertaken by Louis XIV: the decor of the king's mother, Anne d'Autriche's apartments, the Apollo Hall sculpted and painted vault, the enlargement and modernization of the Tuileries palace by Louis Le Vau and the transformation of the Tuileries gardens by André Le Nôtre. After Louis XIV left Paris, the Louvre construction site was left incomplete and the living quarters granted to academic institutions, royal artists or servants.

The furniture and artworks were then moved to other royal abodes, and the grand décors deteriorated, so very few remain today. As early as the 18th century, the Louvre was not as much a royal palace as a "temple of the arts, science and taste". From 1725, a Salon was held there every two years, a major event of the European artistic life, where members of the Academy displayed their works.

The opening of the museum in 1793

Under the reign of Louis XVI, the Louvre started to awake to its vocation as museum, through the project of displaying part of the royal painting collections in the Great Hall to make them accessible to the public. But it was not until the Revolution that the project really came to fruition. After 1791, the Tuileries became the seat of royal power again, after Louis XVI and his family were forcibly taken to Paris. After the fall of the monarchy, the Convention and the executive committees settled in the castle, which remained the main seat of power throughout the 19th century. Then, the museum project designed under Louis XVI finally existed, the museum opening its doors to the public on August 10, 1793. Its collections soon took an unprecedented dimension thanks to the seizing of the Emigrés' estates

The Apollo Gallery.
☞ Department of Decorative Arts, Denon wing, first floor, room 66

and, shortly afterwards, the military campaigns of Napoleon I (the works taken by the Emperor were returned to their countries of origin after his fall in 1815). The Emperor, who had settled in the Tuileries, largely contributed to its florescence with the help of his architects, Charles Percier and Pierre François Léonard Fontaine. Napoleon, who appointed Vivant Denon, artist and diplomat, as the Museum's head, enriched the collections with the acquisition of many antiques from his sister's husband, Prince Borghese. The Egyptian section, meanwhile, developed under the aegis of Charles X and of its first curator, the eminent Egyptologist Jean-François Champollion. From 1852 to 1857, in the context of the business-oriented revamping of Paris by Baron Hausmann undertaken by Napoleon III, the area setting the Louvre apart from the Tuileries was demolished and replaced with a monumental courtyard lined up with modern buildings, designed by Louis Visconti and Hector Lefuel. In this new Louvre, the Rivoli side buildings were held by administrations (first State Departments then the Ministry of Finance after the fall of the Empire), while, on the Seine side, the museum shared space with the Tuileries' utilitarian buildings, such as the royal stalls and the Salle des Etats, devoted to parliamentary sessions.

The Grand Gallery.
☛ Department of Paintings, Denon wing, first floor

From the torments of the Commune to the outside extensions

After the fall of the Second Empire in 1870, the Tuileries palace was set on fire, on orders from General Jules Bergeret of the Paris Forces, during the Bloody Week that marked the defeat of the Paris Commune. Fortunately, the Louvre was left untouched by the fire. The clearing of the ruins in 1883 opened the great perspective from the Louvre to the Place de l'Etoile. During the Interwar Period, the museum underwent, under the tutelage of Henri Verne, Head of National Museums, a radical modernization with the installation of electric lighting and the development of new exhibition spaces (the Sphinx courtyard and Daru stairs). This program was interrupted by World War II, after which the palatial dimension of the building superseded its museum dimension, notably with the recreation, in 1964, of the ditch underneath the Colonnade. During François Mitterrand's presidency, the entire building was finally devoted to the museum collections – the Ministry of Finance leaving the Richelieu wing – and large exhibition spaces ware built to host the public: on March 30, 1989, the Napoleon Hall and architect Ieoh Ming Pei's Pyramid were inaugurated. The latter came to symbolize the Great Louvre, whose finalization owes a great debt to Michel Laclotte, who supervised it from 1987 to 1995.

The Bronzes Hall with its ceiling decorated (*The Ceiling*, 2010) by Cy Twombly (1928-2011).
☛ Department of Greek, Etruscan and Roman Antiquities, Denon wing, first floor, room 32

The museum benefited from an expansion of its orientations and collections with the implementation in 2000 of the Indigenous Arts department, and the creation, in 2003 of a department of Islamic Arts. Under the leadership of Henri Loyrette, President of the Public Establishment from 2001 to 2013, the Louvre has also branched outside the walls of Paris with the Louvre-Lens regional branch, by the SANAA Bureau, and the Abu Dhabi branch by Jean Nouvel. These new extensions bear witness to a history still in the making, confirmed by the inclusion of contemporary art within the institution.

Near Eastern Antiquities

The Near Eastern Antiquities come from 19th century excavations by scholars who went in search of the sources of the Western culture. The reconstitution of the Khorsabad courtyard, with its winged man-headed bulls built to the glory of the Assyrian king Sargon II, asserts the active role of the museum in the rediscovery of the forgotten civilizations of the East. These archaeological discoveries led to the creation of an Assyrian Museum in the Louvre in 1847. Multiple shipments enriched this pioneering research under the auspices of Félicien Saulcy (Turkey, Egypt, Palestine, Syria) or Ernest Renan (Lebanon). Works unearthed from the Sumerian site of Tello in Lower Mesopotamia allowed the creation of a department in 1881. In 1884-1886, Marcel Dieulafoy and his wife led important excavations on behalf of the Louvre in Iran, on the Susa site, capital of the Persian Empire.

Spanning over nine millennia, from prehistoric times to the early Islamic period, the museum tour focuses on three geographical areas organized chronologically. The section on Mesopotamia, which refers to the valley of the Tigris and the Euphrates, the eastern branch of the Fertile Crescent where was born, during the fourth millennium BC, the first urban civilization (the Sumerians, inventors of writing), displays the precious *Code of Hammurabi*, symbolic monument of Babylonian culture. The tour continues with the Persian world, extending to Central Asia and the regions west of the Euphrates, where one can discover the treasures of Susa, including the sublime friezes adorning the palace of Darius I. It closes with the Levant (today's Syria, Lebanon and Israel), to which relate Cyprus, Anatolia, the Arabian Peninsula and North Africa.

Mesopotamia

**Statue of the Official Ebih-Il,
Temple of Ishtar, Mari, Syria,
ca. 2400 BC**
Alabaster, eyes lined with bitumen and
incrusted with shell and lapis-lazuli,
H. 52.5 cm
☞ Richelieu wing, ground floor,
room 1b

This orant-style (meaning "in
prayer") statue was found in
a temple dedicated to Ishtar,
goddess of love and war. The
faithful of the kingdom of
Mari used to cast their effigies
to perpetuate their prayers
before the deity. The dignitary
is portrayed with a certain
amount of naturalism, sitting
on a stool, wearing a *kaunakes*,
his eyes colored with lapis
lazuli.

**Relief of Ur-Nanshe, Prince of Lagash,
Tello, formerly Girsu, state
of Lagash, Iraq, ca. 2500 BC**
Limestone, 39 × 46.5 × 6.5 cm
☞ Richelieu wing, ground floor, room 1a

This punctured bas-relief shows
two scenes, the ceremonies of
foundation and inauguration
of a temple, chaired by the founder
of the first dynasty of Lagash,
Ur-Nanshe. Accompanied by his
butler, dignitaries and members
of his family, the Sumerian ruler
is shown on a scale larger than the
other characters', as a builder King
giving thanks to the gods.

*Victory Stele of Eannatum,
King of Lagash*, called "Stele
of Vultures" ("historic"
side), Tello, ancient Girsu,
State of Lagash, Iraq,
ca. 2450 BC

Limestone, H. 180 cm

☞ Richelieu wing, ground floor,
room 1

These stele fragments retell in words and pictures the
triumphant military campaign of the king of Lagash,
Eannatum, upon the enemies of Umma. One side is
devoted to the narrative of human actions and other,
mythological in nature, to the intercession of the gods.
Although incomplete, this stele is the oldest known
historiographical document.

Mesopotamia

Gudea, Prince of Lagash, with the Gushing Vase,
Tello, ancient Girsu, State of Lagash, Iraq,
ca. 2150 BC
Diorite, H. 62 cm
☛ Richelieu wing, ground floor, room 2

Sumerian Prince of Lagash, Gudea, a very
pious ruler and a builder, devoted much of his
reign to the building or restoration of shrines.
Concerned with the posterity of his name,
he had effigies of him placed on them, such
as this one which shows him holding a vase
of worship, from which flow streams, symbol
of fertility and prodigality.

Kudurru of King Meli-Shipak
commemorating a donation of land to his son
Marduk-apla-iddina, war booty found
in Susa, Iran, 1186-1172 BC
Gray limestone, 65 × 30 cm
☛ Richelieu wing, ground floor, room 3

Hammurabi's death marked a period of
instability in Babylon with the Kassites
dynasty, rulers of foreign origin. To win
the allegiance of strongmen, they made
donations of land, formalized by the
erection of stelae called *Kudurru,* set in
temples to be seen of men and gods. Here,
king Meli-Shipak grants land to his son
Marduk-apla-iddina.

The Code of Hammurabi, Sovereign of Babylon (detail), stele carried off as war booty to Susa, Iran, ca. 1792-1750 BC

Basalt, H. 225 cm

☞ Richelieu wing, ground floor, room 3

Long before the Bible, the *Code of Hammurabi*, in addition to establishing itself as a major historical, literary and artistic work, symbol of the Mesopotamian culture, was the oldest and most complete collection of laws known in the Middle East. At the head of this pillar stands the sun-god of Justice Shamash, recognizable to the flames springing from his shoulders, investing Hammurabi, sixth king of the Amorite dynasty and founder of the first empire of Babylon. The text, spread over the piece in cuneiform writing and Akkadian language, spells out a list of rules and judiciary statements established by the sovereign in all areas of daily and city life (religion, family, slavery, labor, commerce, administration, etc.). Envisioned as a political testament, this stele written in the last years of Hammurabi's life is a unique source of knowledge about one of the most prestigious kingdoms of ancient Mesopotamia.

Near Eastern Antiquities

Capital of the Apadana, Palace of Darius I, Susa, Iran, ca. 510 BC
Limestone, H. 760 cm
☛ Sully wing, ground floor, room 12a

As evidence of the culminating point of the Persian Empire, Darius erected in his capital a grandiose palace, with a courtroom (*Apadana*) punctuated by thirty-six columns. Inspired by Egyptian and Ephesian architecture, they were topped with bull-shaped capitals, replicas of ancient Mesopotamian motifs. This remnant is emblematic of Achaemenid art, based on a combination of different styles to show the unification of the empire.

Frieze of Archers, Susa,
Iran, palace of Darius
the Great, King of Persia,
ca. 500 BC

Enamelled bricks, H. 200 cm
☞ Sully wing, ground floor,
room 12b

This procession of archers depicted in human size
decorated, over several hundred meters, the walls of
Darius' palace. The polychrome glazed bricks found
scattered on the site required a delicate reconstruction
work. The panels figured, in a context of political
unification, the elite corps in the service of the Persian
monarch.

Levant

Idol with Eyes, Northern Syria, ca. 3300-3000 BC
Terracotta, H. 27 cm
☞ Sully wing, ground floor, room C

Found among anthropomorphic platelets with oversized eyes, this curious object, consisting of a bell-shaped body surmounted by a cylindrical neck and two circles of holes, was traditionally linked to these and regarded as an idol. But it is more likely a spinning instrument.

Stele of Baal with a Thunderbolt, Ugarit, Syria, 14th-13th century BC
Limestone, H. 142 cm
☞ Sully wing, ground floor, room B

This stele was discovered at Ugarit, capital of a powerful kingdom of the second millennium BC. Its main patron god, Baal, is portrayed with his left hand grasping a spear from which seeds a small branch. The king of Ugarit, depicted in ceremonial costume, invokes the divinity who calls forth the thunderstorms, essential for agriculture.

Hunt Patera, Temple
of Baal, Ugarit, Syria,
14th-12th century BC
Gold, D. 18.8 cm
☞ Sully wing, ground floor,
room B

The decoration of this cup with a flat bottom and
vertical edges, consists of two friezes, specific to
the international art of the era through its Egyptian,
Aegean and Levantine influences. To the four goats of
the central medallion is superimposed a hunting scene
in which the king of Ugarit hunts bulls and a heifer,
probably symbols of deities.

LE MONDE IRANIEN
ET SES MARGES

DE L'ESPAGNE
À L'ÉGYPTE

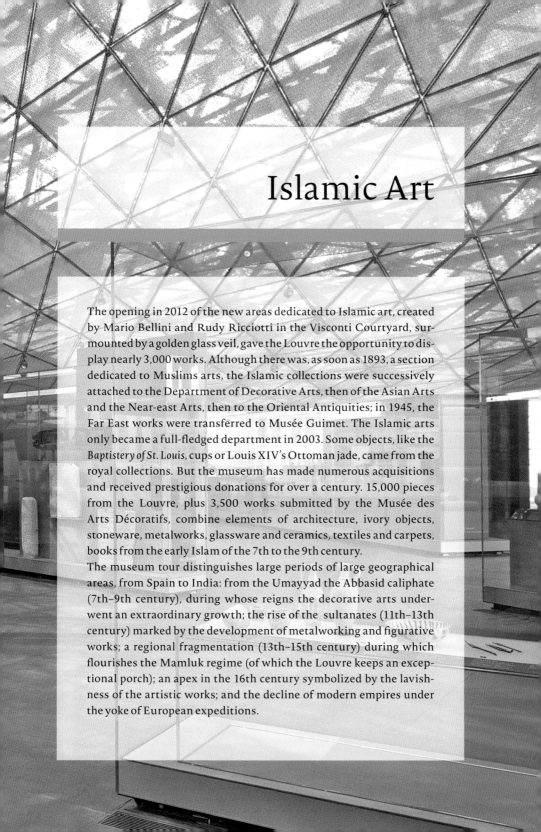

Islamic Art

The opening in 2012 of the new areas dedicated to Islamic art, created by Mario Bellini and Rudy Ricciotti in the Visconti Courtyard, surmounted by a golden glass veil, gave the Louvre the opportunity to display nearly 3,000 works. Although there was, as soon as 1893, a section dedicated to Muslims arts, the Islamic collections were successively attached to the Department of Decorative Arts, then of the Asian Arts and the Near-east Arts, then to the Oriental Antiquities; in 1945, the Far East works were transferred to Musée Guimet. The Islamic arts only became a full-fledged department in 2003. Some objects, like the *Baptistery of St. Louis*, cups or Louis XIV's Ottoman jade, came from the royal collections. But the museum has made numerous acquisitions and received prestigious donations for over a century. 15,000 pieces from the Louvre, plus 3,500 works submitted by the Musée des Arts Décoratifs, combine elements of architecture, ivory objects, stoneware, metalworks, glassware and ceramics, textiles and carpets, books from the early Islam of the 7th to the 9th century.

The museum tour distinguishes large periods of large geographical areas, from Spain to India: from the Umayyad the Abbasid caliphate (7th–9th century), during whose reigns the decorative arts underwent an extraordinary growth; the rise of the sultanates (11th–13th century) marked by the development of metalworking and figurative works; a regional fragmentation (13th–15th century) during which flourishes the Mamluk regime (of which the Louvre keeps an exceptional porch); an apex in the 16th century symbolized by the lavishness of the artistic works; and the decline of modern empires under the yoke of European expeditions.

Egypt, Spain, Iran

Al-Mughira's Pyxis probably Madinat al-Zahra, Cordoba, Spain, 968 AD

Elephant ivory carved and engraved, traces of jet, H. 16 cm, D. 11.8 cm

☛ Denon wing, lower ground floor, room A

This pyxis, carved from a single piece of an elephant's tusk, is an artistic masterpiece. Its iconography, consisting of a profusion of figures and intricate details, reveals its political inspiration: it invites the addressee, Prince Al-Mughira, latest born son of Abd al-Rahman III, Caliph of Spain, to ensure the legitimacy of the Ummayades line against the Abbasids.

Celestial Sphere, by the astrolabe maker Yunus ibn al-Husayn, Baghdad (?), Iraq, or Ispahan, Iran, 1145 AD

Cast copper alloy, engraved and inlaid with silver, D. 16.5 cm

☛ Richelieu wing, ground floor, room 5

Arab scholars distinguished themselves in the sciences and especially astronomy, encouraged by the Abbasid caliphs: knowledge of the heavens was essential, and allowed those who could decipher them to find their way on land and sea. With 1,025 silver pins signaling the stars, this globe, both decorative object and measuring instrument, is the oldest known in the eastern part of the Islamic world.

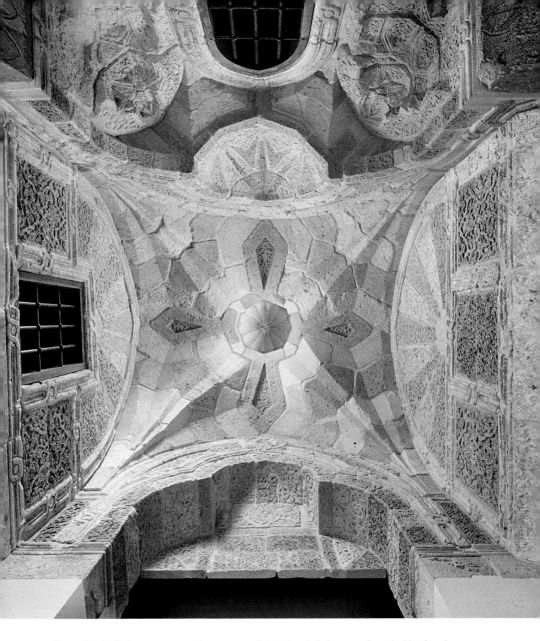

Honor Porch of a home,
from a place called "Qasr
Rumi", Cairo, Egypt,
1475-1500 AD

Carved limestone

☛ Denon wing, ground floor,
room B

A remnant of the Mamluk dynasty founded by freed slave soldiers, that ruled from the 13th to the early 16th century, this porch was the access structure of a prestigious residence in Cairo. Made up of three hundred stones, it is decorated with floral and geometric motifs. There is no other example of a Mamluk building of this size preserved in a museum.

Iran

Shah Abbas I and His Page, signed
by Muhammad Qasim, Iran, 1627
Ink drawing, heightened with color and gold
on paper, 27.5 × 16.8 cm

The most remarkable ruler of the
Safavid dynasty, Abbas I the Great
restored, through his military
victories and reformist politics,
the Iranian supremacy over the
Persian Gulf. But this flourished
miniature portraits him in a more
intimate setting, in a banquet room,
hugging a young cupbearer.

Bowl with Falconer Horseman, Iran,
early 13th century
Siliceous ceramic with a lustred decoration
embellished with gold on opacified glaze,
D. 22 cm
☛ Richelieu wing, lower ground floor,
room 6

Beyond its aesthetic quality, this
cup is the result of a technical
innovation developed in the late
12th century, the *haft rank*, which
means "seven colors" in Persian.
It was baked twice and, the second
time, at a lower temperature
in order to incorporate fragile
pigments and gold highlights.
Iranian potters thus obtained new
nuances of colors.

Carpet with Heavenly Gardens Decor, known as the Mats de Mantes (detail), western Iran (?), Mid-16th century
Cotton warp and weft, wool hair, asymmetric knot, 780 × 385 cm

It is unclear how the carpet came from the East to the collegiate church of Mantes, from which it was named and sold to the Louvre. The pattern of the musket held by the hunter, a weapon that did not appear in Iran till 1528, dates it from the mid-16th century. Various realistic (peacock, lion, deer, etc.) and fantastic animals (dragons and *simurghs*, fabulous birds), make up its flamboyant decor.

Egypt, India, Turkey

Horse Head Dagger, India, 17th century

Steel inlaid with gold, jade and semi-precious stones, W. 50.5 cm

☛ Richelieu wing, lower ground floor, room 11

Its sharp curved blade could have gone through chainmail, but, apart from its fierce efficiency, this dagger, called a *kandjar*, is mostly remarkable for its fine jade handle (famous for helping victory) shaped as a horse head, adorned with emeralds and spinels. This decorative weapon, probably a gift to a high dignitary, is typical of Mughal art.

Bowl, known as the
Baptistery of St. Louis,
made by Muhammad ibn
al-Zayn, Egypt,
early 14th century
Hammered brass, chased and
inlaid with gold, silver and black
paste, H. 23 cm
☛ Denon wing, lower ground
floor, hall B

The Mamluk basin that belonged to the French royal
collections served for the baptism of the future
Louis XIII, but not for St. Louis', who died 50 years
before it was crafted, to whom it is wrongly related by its
nickname. Decorated with scenes dealing with hunting,
power and war, this masterpiece of Islamic metalwork
wears the artist's signature in six different locations.

Peacock Dish,
Iznik, Turkey,
1540-1555 AD
Siliceous ceramic with
decoration painted on slip
and under transparent
glaze, D. 37.5 cm
☛ Denon wing,
ground floor, room B

The development of the saz ornamental
repertoire is largely the work of the painter
and poet Shah Quli, greatly admired
by Sultan Suleiman the Magnificent.
In Ottoman art, *saz* means stylized and
intertwined decorations and plants. The
composition of this dish is characterized
by a balance of masses crafted in nuances
of cobalt blue, turquoise and ultramarine,
characteristic of Iznik ceramics.

Egyptian Antiquities

The interest in Egyptian antiquities enjoyed around the 1800s a significant rise, driven by Bonaparte's expedition and the publications of art historian and Director General of Museums Vivant Denon. But the origin of the Louvre collections really date back to the creation in 1826 of a department devoted to Egypt with, at its head, Jean-François Champollion, who was responsible for the translation of the Pharaonic writing and language through the *Rosetta Stone*. The Central Museum then displayed Egyptian statues from the former royal collections. Under Charles X, many pieces were acquired during major sales or donated to the museum. But in the second half of the 19th century, in addition to the donations, the archaeological missions started to be the main source for the collections, especially under the leadership of Auguste Mariette who, on a mission for The Louvre, unearthed the Serapeum of Saqqara and brought back nearly 6,000 works, including the magnificent *Squatting Scribe*.

The department is organized into three chronological sections. The Pharaonic period, which runs from the fourth millennium to the year 30 BC is the largest one and the richest in artefacts (about 50,000). The museum also holds a large section on Roman Egypt and another on Coptic ("Christianized") Egypt. Beyond their aesthetic qualities, from the sphinx to the famous portraits of Fayum, the Egyptian collections of the Louvre are a unique tool of scientific knowledge on the daily life, culture, beliefs and rites of ancient Egypt.

Egyptian Antiquities

Dagger, Gebel el-Arak (?), in Southern Abydos,
Naqada civilization, ca. 3300-3200 BC
Flint blade, shaft made from the canine tooth of a hippopotamus,
H. 25.5 cm
☛ Sully wing, 1rst floor, room 20

This ceremonial knife, discovered on the site of
Gebel el-Arak, reflects the consummate art of the
early Egyptian sculptors. Its handle, carved out of
the canine tooth of a hippo, displays on both sides
a relatively complex décor, depicting first a combat
on four registers, and secondly a warrior – perhaps a
Mesopotamian deity – holding two lions at bay.

Bull Palette Celebrating a Victory,
Naqada civilization, ca. 3300-3100 BC
Schist, 26.5 × 14.5 cm
☛ Sully wing, 1rst floor, room 20

Naqada, a site of Upper Egypt, saw
the rise, during the Predynastic period,
of the foundations of culture and art
in Egypt. From this early period
remain some vestiges, among which
this fragment of a palette, (called
"historicized") finely carved on
both sides, including, on each side,
a bull trampling a man, symbol
of the victorious king.

*Stele of the Snake King
or the Horus Djet*, royal
necropolis, Abydos,
1rst dynasty, ca. 3000 BC

Limestone, 143 × 65 × 25 cm

☛ Sully wing, 1rst floor,
room 20

On this stele found broken on the site of Abydos, where
lay the rulers of the First Dynasty, can be read the
name of Horus Djet, meaning the "Serpent King": the
hawk, the god Horus' sacred animal, represents the god
embodied on earth by the pharaoh, stands out in relief,
while a snake, one of the most ancient hieroglyphs
known, meaning the cobra, is depicted inside the palace.

Old Kingdom

Egyptian Antiquities

Nefertiabet's Stele, found in the princess' tomb, Giza, Old Kingdom, 9th dynasty, ca. 2590 BC
Painted limestone, 37.5 × 52.5 cm
☛ Sully wing, 1rst floor, room 22

The purpose of this stele was to provide the dead in the afterworld with what was depicted in the image and written on the stone. Sister or daughter of King Khufu, the princess here figured is Nefertiabet, seated and richly adorned, facing the funeral meal offered to her for eternity. In addition to a table covered with food, the stele shows ideograms identifying the items of the offering.

Great Sphinx, Tanis, Old (or Middle) Kingdom, ca. 2600 or 1900 BC
Pink granite, 183 × 480 × 154 cm
☛ Sully wing, lower ground floor, room 1

This twelve tons sphinx, perfectly polished and punctuated by details of a great precision, was exhumed in 1825 from the ruins of the temple of Amun-Ra in Tanis. With a lion's body and a human head, the sphinx is a sovereign creature, ruthless to dissenters and protector of the righteous. The Pharaoh gains, through this depiction, a divine dimension.

 ✳ ❷

Squatting Scribe
**Saqqara, Old Kingdom,
4th or 5th dynasty,
ca. 2620-2350 BC**

Painted limestone, eyes inlaid with
rock crystal and alabaster and ringed
with copper, H. 53.7 cm

☛ Sully wing, 1rst floor, room 20

In an Egypt now equipped with a centralized and complex administration, the function of the scribe is important. An educated man, this official is able to avoid manual labor and participates in national affairs. Although the dedicated qualifier of this scribe designates him as "squatted" or "seated", he actually appears sitting cross-legged. He is depicted at work, his chest slightly tilted forward, an unrolled papyrus on his loincloth used as support, his fingers ready to write with a brush that is now missing. His eyes are made of white red-veined magnesite and polished rock crystal, his eyebrows, aquiline nose and thin lips appear very realistic. Hands, fingers and nails are carved with remarkable delicacy, while his nipples are marked by two wooden pegs. This scribe, his identity still unknown, was discovered in 1850 by archaeologist Auguste Mariette in Saqqara.

Egyptian Antiquities

Hippopotamus Figurine, Middle
Kingdom, ca. 2000-1900 BC
Egyptian faience, glazed laminated
quartz grains, 12.70 × 20.50 × 8.10 cm
☛ Sully wing, 1rst floor, room 23

From a set of objects placed in
a burial vault, this blue faience
hippopotamus, covered with
plants, refers to the Nun, the
primordial swamp where
everything is born. It is a
symbol of rebirth.

*Model of a Boat,
Navigation Scene,*
Middle Kingdom,
ca. 2000 BC
Painted stucco wood,
29.50 × 67 × 15.50 cm
☛ Sully wing, ground
floor, room 3

It was customary to place in the Middle
Empire tombs miniature reproductions
of human activity. Quite fascinating, these
models, in a rudimentary style, vividly bring
back daily life in ancient Egypt: here a boat
ride on the Nile.

Offering-Bearer,
Middle Kingdom,
ca. 1950 BC
Coated and painted ficus
wood, 108 × 14 × 32 cm
☛ Sully wing, 1rst floor,
room 23

This statue of a woman made of twelve pieces
of wood, stood in the vault, bearing on its head
an oxen leg on a trough, to symbolize the food
offerings intended to nourish the deceased in
the afterlife.

Cosmetic Spoon shaped as a swimming young woman, New Kingdom, ca. 1550-1069 BC
Wood, 34 × 7 cm
☛ Sully wing, 1rst floor, room 24

Although this type of object is called a "cosmetic spoon," the actual use of this fragile figurine shaped as a swimming nude young woman bearing waterfowl is uncertain. It may also be an offering spoon or be linked to a fertility cult.

Pendant, Falcon with Ram's Head, found in the tomb of an Apis bull, New Kingdom, 1254 BC
Gold, turquoise, lapis-lazuli, and carnelian cloisonné inlay, 7.10 × 13.70 cm

This jewel, made of 99.5% pure gold, and of precious stones, is a curious animal: the falcon, wings and legs outstretched, displays a ram's head with horizontal horns. It symbolizes the sun which, according to an Egyptian myth, tales this form when it goes down at night in order to regenerate and reappear in the morning.

Fieldwork, **Thebes left bank, today's Luxor, New Kingdom, 18th dynasty, ca. 1450 BC**
Paint and pigment on mud plaster, 68 × 94 cm
☛ Sully wing, 1rst floor, room 4

This evocation of the agrarian life over three registers, reading from bottom to top, used to decorate the tomb of a scribe, in charge of the smooth running of this activity. In addition to preserving the memory of the deceased's life, this painting holds a magical function: it must contribute to the survival of the dead in the afterlife by giving them the resources depicted.

Body of a woman, probably Nefertiti, New Kingdom, ca. 1353-1337 BC
Quartzite, H. 29 cm
☛ Sully wing, 1rst floor, room 25

The headless sculpture exemplifies the art of the el-Amarna period, named from Amarna, a city on the east bank of Middle Egypt in the time of Akhenaten. This torso draws a silhouette both deformed and very sensual, enhanced by the transparent finely pleated draping. Princess Nefertiti, wife of Akhenaten, is often regarded as the model for this bold piece.

King Amenophis IV-Akhenaten, pillar fragment from a building of the east precinct of Karnak, New Kingdom, 18th dynasty, ca. 1353-1337 BC
Painted sandstone, 137 × 88 × 60 cm
☛ Sully wing, 1rst floor, room 25

Akhenaten started an artistic revolution without precedent during his reign, having statues raised depicting him according to a new aesthetic canon. This element of pillar found near a temple dedicated to the sun falcon Re-Horakhty, of whom Pharaoh was the incarnation, is in a position described as "Osirian", arms crossed over his chest and holding the royal scepters.

Stele of Lady Taperet,
**22nd dynasty,
10th or 9th century BC**
Painted wood, 31 × 29 × 2.60 cm
☛ Sully wing, 1rst floor,
room 29

A long-time prerogative of royal tombs, this small
stele, remarkable for its colors and abundant symbolic
elements, bears witness to the outbreak of the funerary
art in the private sphere. It associates the deceased to
the solar cycle. On each of its faces, she prays to the sun
under its two aspects, in the day as the god Ra, at night
as the god Atum.

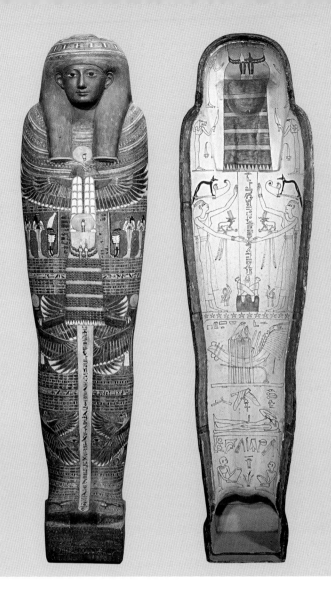

**Lid of Imeneminet's Coffin,
25th-26th dynasties,
ca. 700-600 BC**

Agglomerated and coated fabric,
187 × 48 cm

☛ Sully wing, ground floor,
room 13

The shape of sarcophagi, their use typical of the funerary practices of ancient Egypt in order to protect the body of the dead, evolved considerably over time and across social classes. The front of the sarcophagus, anthropoid, evokes the Abylos reliquary where the head of Osiris was supposedly preserved, while the back shows, through a pillar – the Djed – a relic of the city of Busiris, Osiris' spine. The deceased was thus associated with Osiris, figure of eternity.

Christ and Abbot Mena,
Bawit monastery,
8th century AD
Paint on sycamore fig wood, wax
and distemper, 57 × 57 cm
☞ Denon wing, lower ground
floor, room C

Well preserved, this painting on wood, found on
the Bawit site in Middle Egypt, is the oldest known
Coptic icon – the Coptic being Christians who began
settling in Egypt during the late second century.
It shows at the front, facing a landscape, Christ,
his head haloed in a cruciform nimbus, with the head
monk of a monastery holding a scroll and tracing
a gesture of blessing.

Portrait of a woman, known
as *L'Européenne*, Antinoë (?),
2nd century BC
Encaustic and gilt on a cedarwood
panel, 42 × 24 cm

The Fayum portraits are
named after the region in
which they were found from
1888, sixty kilometers
south of Cairo. It is from
the ruins of a necropolis
that this one was exhumed.
This funeral painting
crafted with encaustic
(the colors diluted in melted
wax) and incorporated
into the mummy (whence
the cut panel, originally
rectangular), proves to be
a portrait in the modern
sense of the term:
the painter sought to
replicate the model in her
individuality.

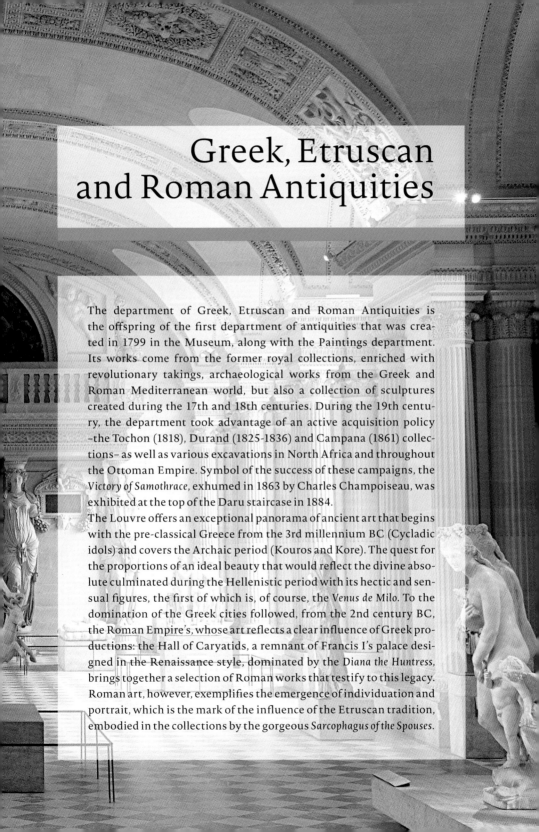

Greek, Etruscan and Roman Antiquities

The department of Greek, Etruscan and Roman Antiquities is the offspring of the first department of antiquities that was created in 1799 in the Museum, along with the Paintings department. Its works come from the former royal collections, enriched with revolutionary takings, archaeological works from the Greek and Roman Mediterranean world, but also a collection of sculptures created during the 17th and 18th centuries. During the 19th century, the department took advantage of an active acquisition policy –the Tochon (1818), Durand (1825-1836) and Campana (1861) collections– as well as various excavations in North Africa and throughout the Ottoman Empire. Symbol of the success of these campaigns, the *Victory of Samothrace*, exhumed in 1863 by Charles Champoiseau, was exhibited at the top of the Daru staircase in 1884.

The Louvre offers an exceptional panorama of ancient art that begins with the pre-classical Greece from the 3rd millennium BC (Cycladic idols) and covers the Archaic period (Kouros and Kore). The quest for the proportions of an ideal beauty that would reflect the divine absolute culminated during the Hellenistic period with its hectic and sensual figures, the first of which is, of course, the *Venus de Milo*. To the domination of the Greek cities followed, from the 2nd century BC, the Roman Empire's, whose art reflects a clear influence of Greek productions: the Hall of Caryatids, a remnant of Francis I's palace designed in the Renaissance style, dominated by the *Diana the Huntress*, brings together a selection of Roman works that testify to this legacy. Roman art, however, exemplifies the emergence of individuation and portrait, which is the mark of the influence of the Etruscan tradition, embodied in the collections by the gorgeous *Sarcophagus of the Spouses*.

Head of female figurine, Keros, 2nd Early Cycladic period, 2700-2300 BC
Marble,
27 × 14.5 × 9.5 cm
☞ Denon wing, lower ground floor, room 1

This head, truncated at the top, surmounted the body of an idol, its arms bent and legs joined together. A remnant of the major artistic center of the Cyclades islands in the third millennium BC, it was decorated with polychrome patterns. Its geometric and sleek shape fascinated 20th century artists such as Modigliani and Brancusi, whose style it largely inspired.

Female Statue, known as The Lady of Auxerre, Crete (?), ca. 640-630 BC
Limestone, H. 75 cm
☞ Denon wing, lower ground floor, room 1

This effigy owes its nickname *The Lady of Auxerre* to the city museum in which it was rediscovered. Its right arm suggests the gesture of a deity pointing at her attributes of fertility, or the worship of a priestess. Its headdress shows the influence of the Egyptian Middle East, while its incised patterns make it a masterpiece of the Daedalic style, referring to the mythical Cretan sculptor Daedalus.

Rider's head said, known as the
Rampin Horseman, Athens, ca. 550 BC
Marble with traces of polychromy, H. 27 cm
☛ Denon wing, lower ground floor, room 1

This head, still imbued with the
sobriety of the archaic style, shows
Eastern influence in the refinement
of its ornaments. Endowed with a
comely face, it figures an Athenian
aristocrat or a victorious athlete,
his hair surmounted by a vegetal
crown. His chest and original mount
are kept in the Acropolis museum
in Athens.

**Euphronios (late 6th century-
first half of the 5th century BC)**
Calyx Crater with red figures, Attica,
ca. 515-510 BC
Terracotta, H. 44.8 cm, D. 55 cm
☛ Sully wing, 1rst floor, room 43

This vase, signed by the famous
painter Euphronios, is emblematic
of the art of red figures ceramics
which appeared in Athens
during the 6th century BC.
This side describes the mythical
battle between Hercules and
Antaeus, son of Gaia, who was
deemed invincible as long as he
remained on the earth, its contact
rejuvenating him. Hercules
defeated him by lifting him up
and choked.

43

Greek, Etruscan and Roman Antiquities

Plate, known as Ergastines Plate: fragment of the eastern frieze of the Parthenon, Athens, 445-438 BC

Marble, 96 × 207 × 12 cm

☛ Sully wing, ground floor, room 6

This fragment of the Parthenon frieze that ran originally on 160 meters around the temple depicts the Ergastines ("female workers" in Greek), responsible for weaving the golden tunic (the *peplos*) offered by the Athenians to their patron goddess, following a harmonious procession. The creation of this bas-relief was overseen by Phidias, the most prestigious sculptor in Antiquity.

Winged Victory of Samothrace, Samothrace, Hellenistic Period, ca. 190 BC

Marble, H. 328 cm

☛ Denon wing, ground floor, Daru staircase

This masterpiece of the Hellenistic period was found during excavations in 1863 on the site of the Sanctuary of the Great Gods in Samothrace, whose cult was known in ancient times to help win naval fights or prevent shipwrecks. Naval battles were indeed many at the time between the great powers to control the Mediterranean. This feminine figure is thus probably an offering and a trophy commemorating a naval victory. Erected at the prow of a ship, it is depicted taken in midair, its wings deployed, its chest proudly arched, its clothes plastered to the body by the spray. Devoid of its head and arms, this *Nike* (Greek for "victory") is nevertheless an unsurpassed example of the sculpture in motion of the 2nd century BC, which expresses at once lyrical vigor and technical mastery, particularly in the draping, and achieves subtle transparency effects.

Greek, Etruscan and Roman Antiquities

* ④

Venus de Milo, Melos,
Hellenistic Period, ca. 100 BC
Marble, H. 202 cm
☛ Sully wing, ground floor, room 16

An aura of mystery shrouds this
mutilated masterpiece, whose
arms were never recovered since
its exhumation in 1820 on the
island of Melos (Milo in Greek),
in south-western Cyclades.
Through their actions or their
attributes, they would have
allowed us to identify the statue.
Its semi nudity and sensual
forms, however, assimilate it to
the goddess of love Aphrodite,
or alternatively Amphitrite, a
marine goddess worshipped in
Melos. In addition to its proud
posture and distant gaze, signs
of divine behavior, this sculpture
displays a unique technical
virtuosity. The shift of its draping
creates many folds beneath
which one guesses the curve of
its legs. Its contrapposto – the
swaying of one leg carrying the
weight of the body – gives a slight
helical motion which increases
its tridimensional dimension.
This jewel of the Louvre Greek
collections sets in marble the
Antique aesthetic ideal, both
classicist and dynamic.

Agasias of Ephesus, son of Dositheus, 2nd century BC, *Warrior Fighter,* known as *The Borghese Gladiator,* Antium, ca. 100 BC

Marble, H. 199 cm

☛ Denon wing, ground floor, room B

This sculpture, signed, on the tree trunk, by Agasias of Ephesus, was rediscovered in the 17th century in Antium and joined the collections of the Borghese family, hence its nickname. It is supposed to be a copy of an original bronze by the famous bronze caster Lysippus of Sicyon. The rotational movement of the fighter mobilizes his musculature in its entirety, making him an idealized model of the male nude.

Hermaphroditos Asleep, **2nd century AD**

Marble, 169 × 89 cm

☛ Sully wing, ground floor, room 17

This Roman copy of a Greek original from the 2nd century BC depicts Hermaphroditos, son of Hermes and Aphrodite who became bisexed after merging with the nymph Salmacis: unhappy to be rejected by the young man, she convinced Zeus to fuse their bodies together. The mattress on which the figure lays was added in the 17th century by the Italian sculptor Bernini.

Etruscan art

Pendant Necklace *shaped as the head of Acheloos,*
Chiusi (?), ca. 480 BC
Gold, H. 36 cm
☞ Denon wing, ground floor, room 19

The collar from the archaic period of
Etruscan art shows a stylized work of gold
and a decorative fantasy that make it a
masterpiece of Etruscan jewelry. Endowed
with protective powers, the pendant figures
Achelous, a river-god from Aetolia, son of
Oceanus and Tethys, with bull attributes
(ears and horns).

Wall Plaque, known as the *Campana Plaque,*
Tomb of Cerveteri (Central Italy),
ca. 530-520 BC
Painted terracotta, H. 118 cm
☞ Denon wing, ground floor, room 18

This plate, found in the Banditaccia
necropolis in Cerveteri, covered the wall of
a tomb. It figures, behind an archer, a winged
genie carrying a woman's soul to the afterlife.
This archaic drawing is characteristic of
Etruscan aesthetic conventions, show some
details (piercing gaze, characters' motions)
specific to the Greek art from Asia Minor.

*Sarcophagus of the Spouses,
a double cinerary urn,
Tomb of Cerveteri
(Central Italy), ca. 510 BC*
Painted terracotta, H. 114 cm
☛ Denon wing, ground floor,
room 18

Called "sarcophagus" because of its exceptional dimensions, this monument is most certainly an urn designed to keep the ashes of a deceased couple. Found in 1845 by the Marquis Campana in the necropolis of Banditaccia, Cerveteri, and purchased in 1861 by Napoleon III, it comes in the form of a bed upon which a man and a woman are half-laid like banqueters, a model from Asia Minor. But, as opposed to Greece where banquets were reserved for men, Etruria placed the woman on an equal level, as evidenced by the representation in the same proportions of both spouses. The wife is shown accomplishing the gesture of offering perfume, an essential component, along with the sharing of wine, of the funeral ritual. The wine-sharing itself is symbolized by the bottle-shaped cushions. Their facial features, very individuated, are endowed with remarkable finesse, while traces of color add to the refinement of the details of hair and cloth.

Greek, Etruscan and Roman Antiquities

Fragment of the Ara Pacis:
Imperial procession, Rome,
13-9 BC
Marble, 114 × 147 cm
☛ Denon wing, ground floor

This fragment from the altar of Peace erected in honor of Emperor Augustus was inspired by the famous Panathenaic frieze made for the Parthenon temple. Inspired by Greek art, this propaganda-oriented decor portrays the dignitaries of the Empire and the Emperor's family, preceded by Augustus himself, epitomized as the keeper of the world's stability.

Goblet with skeletons, Boscoreale treasure,
near Pompeii, 1st century AD
Gilded silver, H. 10.4 cm
☛ Sully wing, 1rst floor, room 33

The remains buried by the eruption of the Vesuvius in 79 AD reflect the lifestyle of rich Roman citizens. From the Boscoreale villa, located not far from Pompeii, was excavated a treasure consisting of table and toilet utensils, made up precious materials, their designs inspired by mythology or history.

The Emperor Hadrian, Heraklion, ca. 127-128 AD

Marble, H. 64 cm

☞ Denon wing, ground floor, room 25

Famous for his consolidation and the building of a peaceful balance of the Roman Empire in the early 2nd century, Hadrian is also considered a great patron of the arts and literature. This official bust shows him wearing a breastplate decorated with the head of Medusa, a Greek pattern; the iris of his eyes are carved, a novel feature.

Fragment of mosaic floor: The Triumph of Neptune and Amphitrite, Constantine, first quarter of the 4th century AD

Marble, limestone and glass paste, 836 × 714 cm

Rich villas of the Late Antiquity were commonly decorated with mosaics bearing, as if they were carpets, complex patterns in elegant colors. This abundant pavement, found in the reception room of a home in Algeria, figures the triumph of the God of the sea, accompanied by his wife Amphitrite, on a chariot pulled by sea horses and framed by Cupids.

Paintings

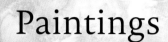

The paintings collections of the museum find their origin in the successive acquisitions of French kings, begun in the reign of Francis I. These formed the basis of the Museum collections, opened to the public in 1793, later expanded through military campaigns and acquisitions at Salons or from individuals, but also donations (most notably from La Caze, Moreau-Nélaton, Rothschild or, more recently, Lemme, Kaufmann and Schlageter). From the first floor of the Denon wing to the second floor of the Court Square and the Richelieu wing, the museum's paintings illustrate the great movements of European art from the 13th century to the mid-19th century. The works posterior to the revolution of 1848 were moved to the Musée d'Orsay in 1986. The Italian Renaissance, marked by the rediscovery of the ancient canons, and an increased attention to nature and its laws, a sense of idealization and a great sensuality, displays its most emphatic testimonies with the *Mona Lisa* by Leonardo Vinci and *The Wedding Feast at Cana* by Veronese. During the 17th century, the classical French style (Poussin, Champaigne) flourished, characterized by a research of purity and harmony, while the Flemish (Rubens) and Dutch (Rembrandt) paintings bloomed in a more naturalistic endeavour. The 18th century, rich in lascivious or even libertine productions (Boucher, Fragonard), saw the emergence of a neo-classical style, based on a strict organization of forms which led to further historical and rigorous compositions such as the famous *Coronation of the Emperor Napoleon* by David, which was answered by a more romantic sentimentalism, especially embodied by the *Liberty Leading the People* by Delacroix.

14th century-16th century

Painter working in Paris
Portrait of John the Good, King of France,
ca. 1360
Tempera on wood, 60 × 44.5 cm
☛ Richelieu wing, 2nd floor, room 1

The model of this rare easel painting
of the 14th century is, according
to the inscription above his head,
John II, before he became king of
France. Indeed, he is shown crownless,
over a gold background and by side,
as on the medals of the time.
This anonymous work is the earliest
known individualized portrait
in Western painting.

Jean Fouquet
(ca. 1415/1420-1477-1450)
Portrait of Charles VII, King of France,
ca. 1445-1450
Tempera on wood, 85.7 × 70.6 cm
☛ Richelieu wing, 2nd floor, room 6

This frontal portrait at the waist
depicts Charles VII, who defeated
the English during the Hundred
Years War, with the help of Joan
of Arc. This work to the glory of the
sovereign, by the famous painter
and miniaturist Jean Fouquet, is
considered, because of its refined and
realistic construction, as the flagship
of early French Renaissance.

Jean Clouet (1490/1495-1540-1541)(attributed to)
Portrait of François I,
King of France, ca. 1530
Oil on wood, 96 × 74 cm
☛ Richelieu wing, 2nd floor, room 7

To picture Francis I, acknowledged as a prodigal and enlightened patron of the arts, Jean Clouet, the king's official painter, uses (with the probable collaboration of his son Francis), the same composition as Fouquet, with a mid-body posture and a frontal intake. The smile, the position of hands, the sumptuous clothing are reminiscent of the influence of Italian painting, of which the king was very fond.

**Attributed to Jean Malouel
(prior to 1370-1415)**
Pietà, known as the *Large Round
Pietà*, ca. 1400
Tempera on wood, D. 64 cm
☞ Richelieu wing, 2nd floor, room 3

Painted for Philip the Bold,
Duke of Burgundy, this Pietà,
which concentrates a wide
range of emotions, associates
the theme of the Man of
Sorrows with the Trinity. In a
small space, Jesus down from
the Cross and supported by
angels, God the Father with
the Dove of the Holy Spirit,
Mary Magdalene and John
the Evangelist crying (right),
are gathered.

Enguerrand Quarton (documented from 1444 to 1466)
Pietà of Villeneuve-lès-Avignon, ca. 1455
Tempera on wood, 163 × 218.5 cm
☞ Richelieu wing, 2nd floor, room 4

This masterpiece of the Provençal School was attributed to Enguerrand Quarton, from Picardy and schooled in the north of France. There, silhouetted against a golden background, where radiates, remote, the heavenly Jerusalem, appear John the Evangelist, a dead Christ treated with a chilling naturalism, a Virgin Mary, aged by pain, and Mary Magdalene. On the left, the donor, an unidentified Canon in white surplice, is depicted at the same scale as the holy characters.

Henri Bellechose (documented from 1415 to his death ca. 1440/1444)
Altarpiece: Martyrdom of St. Denis, 1416
Gilt background from wood to canvas, 162 × 211 cm
☞ Richelieu wing, 2nd floor, room 3

John the Fearless's official painter, Duke of Burgundy, Bellechose completed this altarpiece for the church of the Champmol monastery. Final testimony of the Gothic aesthetics, this work is dominated by a gold background, shades of blue and bloody red traces to glorify the value of sacrifice. To the martyrdom of Jesus, it superimposes St. Denis'. Two episodes are thus told: communion in prison, left, and decapitation, right.

French Painting

**Jean Cousin the Elder
(ca. 1490-ca. 1560)**
Eva Prima Pandora,
ca. 1550
Wood, 97 × 150 cm
☛ Richelieu wing, 2nd floor, room 9

Representative of the school of Fontainebleau, Cousin signs here one of the first nudes of French painting in the continuity of the Venetian model as formulated by Giorgione and Titian. The identity of this woman, both Eve, the first human woman who birthed sin, and Pandora, a mythological figure who spread evil on Earth, is doubly associated with evil.

**Fontainebleau
school,** *Gabrielle
d'Estrées and one of
her sisters in the bath,*
ca. 1595
Oil on wood, 96 × 125 cm
☛ Richelieu wing, 2nd floor, room 10

This enigmatic painting is characteristic of the school of Fontainebleau, particularly of its taste for *trompe-l'œil.* Two sisters pose nude in a bathtub: the Duchess of Villars, left, pinches the breast of Gabrielle d'Estrées, mistress of Henri IV, pregnant with the king's natural child and holding a ring, token of faithfulness. In the background, a young woman sews, perhaps a layette for the unborn child.

Fontainebleau school,
Diana the Huntress, ca. 1550
Oil on canvas, 191 × 132 cm
☛ Richelieu wing, 2nd floor, room 9

This representation is inspired by a *Diana with Doe*, a Hellenistic sculpture, of which a bronze-cast by Primaticcio was kept in Fontainebleau. The goddess of the hunt, accompanied by a greyhound is, under the guise of mythological evocation, a pretext for a sensual nude, probably an idealized portrait of Diane de Poitiers, mistress of King Henry II.

French Painting

Georges de La Tour (1593-1652)
The Repentant Magdalena,
ca. 1640-1645
Oil on canvas, 128 × 94 cm
☞ Sully wing, 2nd floor, room 28

A favorite theme of Georges de La Tour, the meditation of Mary Magdalena before the flame of a candle, hand resting on a skull (a sign of vanity), refers to human frailty. This painting, of extreme formal purity and composed in a very limited range of ocher, is above all one of the most successful variations of chiaroscuro in the history of art.

Lubin Baugin (vers 1612-1663)
Still Life with Chessboard, ca. 1631
Oil on canvas, 55 × 73 cm
☞ Sully wing, 2nd floor, room 27

This still life, attributed to Lubin Baugin, can be interpreted as an allegory of the five senses or an allegory of the "two loves", namely profane – the pleasures of carnal love – and sacred – religious life. The virtuoso artist makes the materiality of things felt, while portraying their futile and ephemeral nature.

Georges de La Tour,
*The Cheat with the ace
of diamonds*, Lunéville,
ca. 1635

Oil on canvas, 107 × 146 cm
☞ Sully wing, 2nd floor,
room 28

This painting is one of the first by the forgotten painter
Georges de La Tour to have been rediscovered in the
20th century. It deals with a favorite theme
of Caravaggio-inspired painting, a game of prime,
the ancestor of poker. The movement of glances between
the courtesan, the maid and the player on the left, who
turns to the beholder as to associate them with their cheat,
reflects their complicity against the boy on the right.

French Painting

Nicolas Poussin
(1594-1665)
Self-Portrait or *Portrait*
of the artist, 1650
Oil on canvas, 98 × 74 cm
☞ Richelieu wing, 2nd floor,
room 14

Acknowledged as the greatest example of French
classicism in the 17th century, although most of his
career took place in Italy, Poussin is here in his studio
as a model of authority. To the left of the composition,
figures, like a painting within a painting, an allegory
of painting embraced by the arms of friendship.

**Nicolas Poussin
(1594-1665)**
*Spring or Paradise Lost;
Summer or Ruth et Boaz;
Autumn or Grapes from
the Promised Land;
Winter or The Flood,*
ca. 1660-1664
Oil on canvas, 118 × 160 cm
☛ Richelieu wing, 2nd floor,
room 16

The *Four Seasons* by Poussin are four scenes of Sacred
History. Spring is figured through Eden; the episode
of Boaz and Ruth evokes summer; a cluster of grapes
from the Promised Land illustrates the fall, and finally
the flood symbolizes winter. These landscape paintings
culminate to a vision of the divine and the sacred.

Philippe de Champaigne (1602-1674)

Ex-Voto of 1662, 1662

Oil on canvas, 165 × 229 cm

☞ Sully wing, 2nd floor, room 24

In gratitude for the healing of his daughter Catherine, who recovered the use of her legs through the prayers of Mother Angelique Arnauld, Philippe de Champaigne, court portraitist and great religious painter, offered this ex-voto to the Port Royal Jansenist convent. This eminent representative of French classicism demonstrates here an exemplary economy of means in the composition and choice of colors.

Claude Gellée, known as le Lorrain (ca. 1602-1682)
The Disembarkation of Cleopatra at Tarsus,
1642-1643
Oil on canvas, 119 × 170 cm
☞ Richelieu wing, 2nd floor, room 15

At first glance, this work tells the story of Cleopatra's landing in the port of Tarsus to win over Marc-Antoine to Egyptian interests. In reality, far from worrying about historical realism, Lorrain, a major figure of French landscape painting, stages a whimsical scene in which he paints the subtle radiance of a sunset over the sea.

Louis (or Antoine?) Le Nain (ca. 1600/ 1610-1648)
Family of Peasants Indoors,
ca. 1640-1645
Oil on canvas,
113 × 159 cm
☞ Sully wing, 2nd floor, room 29

Along with the painting of the "grand topics", depictions of everyday common life developed in France during the early 17th century, as evidenced by this iconic "peasant" painting by the Le Nain brothers. Rediscovered in the 19th century, they excelled to transcend naked reality. In front of a fire the members of a modest family are gather; a child, center, is playing the flute.

French Painting

Nicolas de Largillière (1656-1746)
Family Portrait,
ca. 1710
Oil on canvas,
149 × 200 cm
☛ Sully wing, 2nd floor, room 35

A very sought after portraitist in his time, Largillière, thanks to his mastery of material effects, gives brilliance, poise and elegance to his models. However, as evidenced by the attitude of the girl among her relatives, his art is also characterized by the introduction of a more vibrant and modern natural spontaneity.

Charles Le Brun (1619-1690)
Pierre Séguier, Chancellor Séguier,
ca. 1655-1657
Oil on canvas, 295 × 351 cm
☛ Sully wing, 2nd floor, room 32

It is through the patronage of Chancellor Séguier that Le Brun was able to go learn his trade in Rome. The future First Painter to the King and director of the Royal Academy of Painting and Sculpture paints here his patron, without any frills, riding majestically on a cloudy sky background. The artist is depicted as the groom holding the umbrella.

**Hyacinthe Rigaud
(1659-1743)**
Portrait of Louis XIV, 1701
Oil on canvas, 277 × 194 cm
☞ Sully wing, 2nd floor,
room 34

The official portrait painter of Louis XIV, Rigaud gives
with this particular portrait of the king in his coronation
robes, at the age of sixty-three, the image of absolutism
and royal majesty. Commissioned for the grand-son
of the monarch, King of Spain, the painting remained,
due to its quality, at the court of France.

French Painting

Jean Siméon Chardin (1699-1779)
Saying Grace, ca. 1740
Oil on canvas, 49 × 39 cm
☛ Sully wing, 2nd floor, room 40

Chardin reinterprets a theme very popular among the masters of the 17th century Dutch painting: a mother teaches her two daughters to recite their prayers before eating. This genre, the capture of a daily moment of intimacy, set in a bare frame and achieved with a great economy of means, was an immediate success.

Jean Siméon Chardin (1699-1779)
The Ray, prior to 1728
Oil on canvas, 114 × 146 cm
☛ Sully wing, 2nd floor, room 38

Chardin's reception work at the Royal Academy of Painting and Sculpture, this work marks the beginning of the master of the still life. Around a pyramidal construction made up of a skinned ray fish, revolves an assemblage of organisms – cat, oysters, fish – and domestic utensils. Objects are "so true they deceive the eye," wrote Diderot.

**Jean Antoine Watteau
(1684-1721)**
*Pilgrimage to the Isle
of Cythera*, Paris, 1717
Oil on canvas, 129 × 194 cm
☞ Sully wing, 2nd floor,
room 36

With this painting, Watteau joined the prestigious
Royal Academy of Painting. His lively, sometimes
dazzling, touch, stages lovers leaving Cythera, a Greek
island devoted to love and the pleasures of Aphrodite.
This sweet seduction scene is emblematic of the bucolic
genre called "fête galante" invented by the painter.

French Painting

Jean-Baptiste Greuze
(1725-1805)
The Village Bride, 1761
Oil on canvas, 92 × 117 cm
☛ Sully wing, 2nd floor, room 51

Readily inclined to sentimental
and moralistic genre painting,
Greuze treats here the theme of
the loss of virginity with a clever
ambiguity. The girl's candid look
contrasts with the broken jug
hanging from her arm, the flowers
scattered among her dress and her
hands that seem to point at her
pubis.

**Jean Honoré Fragonard
(1732-1806)**
The Bolt, ca. 1778
Oil on canvas, 73 × 93 cm
☛ Sully wing, 2nd floor,
room 48

While the gesture of closing the lock suggests the lover is about to "take" the woman, an apple, symbol of sin, placed on the table in the alcove, the messy aspect of the room seems to indicate an act already consummated. Renowned for his libertine scenes, Fragonard emphasizes, through temporal jamming, the disorder and violence of the senses, heralding a pre-romantic inspiration.

**François Boucher
(1703-1770)**
*Diana leaving
her bath*, 1742
Oil on canvas, 56 × 73 cm
☛ Sully wing, 2nd floor,
room 38

The huntress Diana relaxes near a water pond with a bathing woman, looking at her foot. A bare leg has a great value in the 18th century erotic aesthetics, and Boucher was reputed for his ability to give a vibrant sparkle to the flesh. This master of gallant and rococo painting enjoyed a great success during his lifetime, especially with Madame de Pompadour.

French Painting

Jacques Louis David (1748-1825)
Madame Récamier, 1800
Oil on canvas, 174 × 244 cm
☞ Denon wing, 1rst floor, room 75

Although unfinished, this painting offers a model of ideal beauty. The frame, spare, shows Juliette Recamier, a learned woman whose salon was the center of social life of her time. Leader of neoclassicism, David depicts with accuracy the elements and the fashionable Antique-style clothing, all signs of a revival of social, political and aesthetic values.

Hubert Robert (1733-1808)
La Salle des Saisons au Louvre, ca. 1802
Oil on canvas, 37 × 46 cm
☞ Sully wing, lower ground floor, room 1

Hubert Robert excels in the representation of architecture, which he renders with a spectacular realism, but sometimes rearranges according to his fancy, often imagining buildings in ruins. Here, he painted the salle des Saisons of the Louvre, opened in 1800. Among the masterpieces present, we may recognize the *Crouching Venus* and *Diana the Huntress* in the foreground, and the *Laocoon* in the background.

**Élisabeth Vigée-Lebrun
(1755-1842)**
*Madame Vigée-Lebrun
and Her Daughter,* 1789
Wood, 130 × 94 cm
☛ Denon wing, 1rst floor,
room 75

In a time when women's access to artistic trades
was particularly difficult, Élisabeth Vigée-Lebrun,
Marie-Antoinette's official portraitist, figured an
uplifting exception. Picturing herself with her daughter
dressed in the Antique style, she exalts, in a spare and
lightweight style inspired by David, the feeling of family
tenderness.

 6

Jacques Louis David,
*Coronation of Napoleon I
in Notre-Dame*, 1806-1807
Oil on canvas, 621 × 979 cm
☞ Denon wing, 1rst floor, room 75

Once the champion of the
French Revolution, David
was appointed in 1804, First
Painter to the Emperor.
It fell to him to set to
memory the coronation of
December 2nd, 1804, during
which Bonaparte became
Napoleon I. But instead of

the Emperor's crowning,
he chose to illustrate his
wife Josephine's. His huge
– almost ten meters wide –
and extremely precise
composition deploys a
long frieze of figures – one
hundred ninety-one,
including the artist himself

shown drawing among
the stands – gathered in
the choir Notre Dame
under the gaze of Pope
Pius VII. This propaganda
commission does not
preclude some reinventions:
Napoleon's mother, figured
here among the audience,

had actually declined to
attend. This demonstration
of David's genius – "we
are truly walking inside
this painting," said the
emperor – who managed
to offer a sumptuous show
without succumbing to
grandiloquence or blister,

offers a manifesto for the
grand French tradition,
based on renewal of
classicism and political
commitment.

French Painting

Eugène Delacroix
(1798-1863)
The 28th of July 1830.
Liberty guiding the people,
1830
Oil on canvas, 260 × 325 cm
☞ Denon wing, 1rst floor,
room 77

This painting, filled with a truly epic passion,
illustrates the Three Glorious Days, revolutionary
days of 1830 led by the people of Paris against
Charles to put an end to the Restoration. Delacroix,
who was not himself a follower of political violence,
nevertheless achieved, with this work, the allegory
of resistance and struggle for justice. In the midst
of a crowd gathering people of all social origins,
a woman, half naked, adorned with a Phrygian cap
and holding a blue-white-red banner (prohibited under
the Restoration), symbolizes Liberty and embodies
the dream of a victory over despotism. The leader
of the romantic artistic movement manages here a
successful synthesis of realism and idealism. Despite
an enthusiastic reception at the Salon of 1831 and its
purchase by the government, this painting was long
hidden because of its message deemed too subversive
by King Louis-Philippe under the July Monarchy.

**Théodore Géricault
(1791-1824)**
The Raft of the Medusa, 1819
Oil on canvas, 491 × 716 cm
☛ Denon wing, 1rst floor,
room 77

This painting by Gericault, considered as the manifesto
of the Romantic School, reinterprets the canons of
history painting through the treatment of actuality:
in 1816, a French frigate sunk off the coast of Senegal
because of the incompetence of its commander. The
painting blends a macabre register – the shipwrecked
seamen die or plunge into madness – and the lyricism
of hope: a mulatto mounted on a barrel waves to a boat
in the horizon.

French Painting

**Eugène Delacroix
(1798-1863)**
*Women of Algiers
in their apartment,*
1834
Oil on canvas,
180 × 229 cm
☛ Denon wing,
1rst floor, room 77

Delacroix had the chance to travel
through North Africa and the Orient. This
painting derives from a visit to a harem,
a rare privilege. It thus appears as both a
kind of document at the heart of sweet
and sieved intimacy, and a painting of
great sensuality, where the poses and
glances build a kind of arabesque.

Eugène Delacroix
(1798-1863)
The Death of Sardanapalus,
1827
Oil on canvas, 392 × 496 cm
☞ Denon wing, 1rst floor,
room 77

This painted, misunderstood and maligned by the
defenders of classicism, caused an uproar when it was
displayed at the Salon of 1828, very late as Delacroix
took some time to complete it. It depicts, in shimmering
tones, a terrible scene: an Assyrian king, certain of his
death during a sacking, rules that none of his riches may
survive him. He orders his properties burnt, his wives,
slaves and cattle, slain.

Jean Auguste
Dominique Ingres
(1780-1867)
La Grande Odalisque,
1814
Oil on canvas, 91 × 162 cm
☞ Denon wing,
1rst floor, room 75

Ingres never made the trip to the East,
but he nevertheless yielded to the orientalist
fad. When he composed paintings about
this theme, he used his own personal
projections. Here, he combines a few signs
of Ottoman inspiration – hookah, turban... –
with this woman whose anatomy appears
distorted. To give this sensual curve, Ingres
gave her three extra vertebrae!

French Painting

Hippolyte Flandrin
(1809-1864)
Nude Youth Sitting
By The Sea, Study, 1837
Oil on canvas, 98 × 124 cm
☞ Sully wing, 2nd floor,
room 63

Ingres' favorite student, Flandrin, proved, like himself, to possess a unique feel for the drawn line. This painting was composed while he was a resident at the Academy of Rome; it shows a man curled up on himself, on the edge of a cliff, in a melancholy posture. The Mediterranean landscape and the accent on the blue and the green confer to this enigmatic nude some kind of ideal beauty.

Jean Auguste Dominique Ingres (1780-1867)
The Turkish Bath, 1862
Oil on canvas, D. 108 cm
☞ Sully wing, 2nd floor, room 60

Ingres only completed this painting at the end of his career. Sold in a rectangular format in 1859 to a cousin of Napoleon III, it is the result of a long process of reworks and research, particularly on the subject of bathers: his famous *Baigneuse de Valpinçon* served as a template for the woman shown from the back, lighted by a delicate beam. With this fantastical vision of a Turkish harem crawling with lascivious bodies in a heady atmosphere, the artist offers us the apex of his art.

Italian Painting

Cenni di Pepi, known as Cimabue (documented from 1272 to 1302)
The Virgin and Child in Majesty surrounded by six angels, ca. 1270
Tempera on wood, 427 × 280 cm
☛ Denon wing, 1rst floor, room 3

This type of iconography, in which the Virgin and Christ, facing the audience, stand in majesty is called *Maesta*. Six angels surround them. This monumental work, with a sumptuous gold background, was painted by Cimabue, a major Florentine artist of the late 13th century, standing between the Byzantine tradition, with its hieratic aesthetics, and the style of the early Renaissance in which more sensitivity and humanity come to life.

Simone Martini (ca. 1284-1344)
The Carrying of the Cross, ca. 1335
Tempera on wood, 28 × 16 cm
☛ Denon wing, 1rst floor, room 4

A brilliant example of Sienese Gothic painting, Martini depicts here a transitional episode in the Passion of Christ: sentenced to death, he walks to the Golgotha carrying his cross. Around him are his tormentors and his family, crowned, among whom the Virgin, John and Madeleine. This vivid scene is endowed with a refined composition that combines graphic rhythms, a search for depth and shimmering colors.

Giotto di Bondone
(ca. 1267-1337)
St Francis of Assisi receiving the stigmate,
ca. 1295-1300

Tempera on wood,
313 × 163 cm

☛ Denon wing,
1rst floor, room 3

Giotto, who intensifies the expressions and dedicates a particular attention to the naturalism of decor, deeply renewed Florentine painting through the introduction of volume and spatial depth, making him, in a way, the "father" of Renaissance. A hermit living on prayer, St. Francis receives from the Christ, who appears in the heavens in the shape of seraph, five wounds: the stigmata of the crucified.

Italian Painting

Guido di Pietro,
known as Fra Angelico
(ca. 1395/1400-1455)
The Coronation of the Virgin,
ca. 1430-1435

Tempera on wood, 209 × 206 cm

☞ Denon wing, 1rst floor,
room 3

About Fra Angelico, Michelangelo said he must have visited heaven before coming back to earth to be able to describe the sacred world so accurately. But Fra Angelico, a professional painter in the Gothic tradition who had donned the cloth, also proves very modern, multiplying optical devices in order to create a sense of perspective.

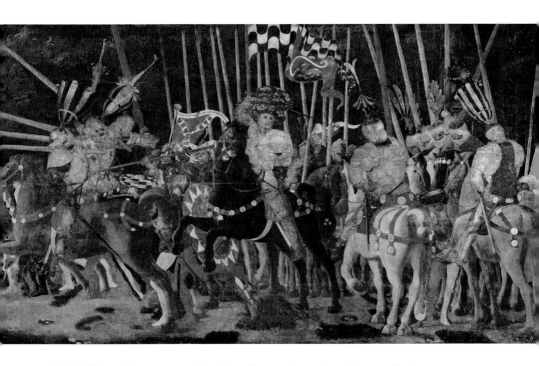

Paolo di Dono, known as Uccello (1397-1475)
The Battle of San Romano: the counter-attack by Micheletto da Cotignola, ca. 1455-1456
Tempera on wood, 182 × 317 cm
☞ Denon wing, 1rst floor, room 3

Uccello, an innovative genius who nevertheless managed to remain faithful to Gothic aesthetics, refers, on this decorative panel commissioned by Cosimo de Medici, the battle between the troops of Florence and Siena in 1432. Although the artist succeeds in giving the scene depth through the contrast in scale between the entangled figures. The painting, however, keeps an overall aspect of dehumanization and unreality.

Italian Painting

Domenico di Tommaso Bigordi, known as Ghirlandaio (1449-1494)
Portrait of an old man and little boy, ca. 1488
Tempera on wood, 63 × 46 cm
☛ Denon wing, 1rst floor, room 5

Managing a major workshop in Florence in the late 15th century, Ghirlandaio signs here a reflection on the ages of life by picturing this old man whose unsightly looks contrast with the freshness of the child. This work is distinguished by the quality of the color contrasts, the delicacy of the landscape in the background and the depth of the facial expressions.

Antonio di Puccio di Cerreto or Antonio Pisano, known as Pisanello (before 1395-1455)
Portrait of a Princess of Este, ca. 1436-1438
Oil on wood, 43 × 30 cm
☞ Denon wing, 1rst floor, room 4

Piero della Francesca (ca. 1416/1417-1492)
Portrait of Sigismondo Malatesta, ca. 1451
Oil on wood, 44 × 34 cm
☞ Denon wing, 1rst floor, room 4

Antonello da Messina (ca. 1430-1479)
Portrait of a man, known as *Le Condottiere*, 1475
Oil on wood, 36.2 × 30 cm
☞ Denon wing, 1rst floor, room 5

During the Quattrocento, the iconographic research aiming at depicting the human figure increased exponentially. Portraits by Pisanello and Piero della Francesca feature side views, remindful of the medallions' traditional patterns, but with a great deal of pictorial details (complexion, beauty clothes, decorations). With Antonello da Messina, who masters all the technical virtues of oil painting as a true virtuoso, the face is taken at a three quarters angle, to achieve an effect of remarkable acuity. The reliefs of the bone structure, the brightness of the eyes, and the rendering of the hair distribution, give the model a solid presence.

Italian Painting

Pietro di Cristoforo Vannucci, known as Perugino (ca. 1450-1523)
Apollo and Marsyas, ca. 1495
Tempera on wood, 39 × 29 cm

From the Umbrian province, Perugino ruled over two important workshops in Florence and Perugia. Here, the painter depicts the musical contest that pitted the god Apollo against the young satyr Marsyas. The work on the accurate proportions and grace of the naked body reminds how deeply the Renaissance was marked by a concern with Antique ideals.

Andrea Mantegna (1431-1506)
St. Sebastian, ca. 1480
Tempera on canvas, 255 × 140 cm
☞ Denon wing, 1rst floor, room 5

Martyrized for his Christian faith, Sebastian is here tied to a column, pierced by arrows. Mantegna depicts him with a muscular body, his eyes turned skyward. The scenery, teeming with ancient ruins which were being rediscovered in Italy at the time, reflects the archaeological culture of the artist and his taste for illusionist effects.

**Sandro di Mariano
Filipepi, known as
Botticelli (ca. 1445-1510)**
*Venus and the Graces offering
gifts to a young woman*
(detail), ca. 1480-1483
Fresco, 211 × 283 cm
☞ Denon wing, 1rst floor,
room 1

This fresco from the Villa Lemmi, near Florence, reflects
the elegance of the Botticellian art, all in the sensual
curves and delicate colors. Heavily influenced by the
humanism of the Renaissance, Botticelli imbues his
mythological subject with Neoplatonic theories. Venus,
accompanied by the Graces, presents a gift to a young
girl, symbolizing an accession to Beauty itself.

Italian Painting

Leonardo da Vinci (1452-1519)
John the Baptist, ca. 1516-1517
Oil on wood, 69 × 57 cm
☛ Denon wing, 1rst floor, room 5

It is probably Salai, Leonardo's assistant, who was the model for this figure with a disarmingly beautiful smile. Beyond the stroke of genius of the index finger pointing at the sky, signaling the advent of the Savior, the emergence of the shadow in the light of John the Baptist establishes Leonardo's mastery of the chiaroscuro.

Leonardo da Vinci (1452-1519)
Portrait of Lisa Gherardini del Giocondo, known as *La Giaconda or Mona Lisa*, ca. 1503-1506
Oil on wood, 77 × 53 cm
☛ Denon wing, 1rst floor, room 6

The unique fate of this masterpiece has become legend. Interpreted and parodied over and over again, the *Mona Lisa* is, in all likelihood, the result of a commission for a portrait painted in Florence between 1503 and 1506: that of Lisa Gherardini, wife of Francesco del Giocondo, a Florentine cloth merchant. It was however never delivered to its sponsors: the painter, who regarded it as unfinished, took it with him to France, and his disciple Salai brought it back to Italy after his death. It is unclear how the painting finally entered the collections of Francis I. Although the identity of the model remains controversial – some even see an androgynous self-portrait – the *Mona Lisa* has nevertheless embodied a type of feminine ideal. Her extremely pure face is livened up by an enigmatic smile which contributed to her mythic aura. The model, captured at mid-body, in a three-quarters angle, is seating before a loggia; in the back, lays an imaginary landscape, as a transition from the earthly to the heavenly.

Italian Painting

**Leonardo da Vinci
(1452-1519)**
*The Virgin and
Child with St Anne,*
unfinished work,
ca. 1508-1510
Oil on wood, 168 × 130 cm
☞ Denon wing, 1rst floor,
room 5

Leonardo's famous *sfumato* wraps this
uncommon scene with a subtle mist,
inherited from the Middle Ages: the Virgin
is portrayed sitting on the lap of her mother
Anne, with the Child who is playing with a
lamb, a symbol of his upcoming martyrdom.
The pyramidal construction is offset by
the roundness of lines giving the feeling
of family tenderness.

Raffaello Sanzio, known as Raphael (1483-1520)
Virgin and Child with St. John the Baptist, known as *La Belle Jardinière,* 1507
Oil on wood, 122 × 80 cm
☞ Denon wing, 1rst floor, room 5

Regarded as a model of its kind, this Madonna and Child of Raphael's Florentine period offers a bucolic scene that seems more maternal than religious. Often opposed to Michelangelo as the other giant of the Italian Renaissance, Raphael was later proclaimed one of the favorite artists of the papal power, contributing to its prestige with his monumental frescoes in the Vatican.

Italian Painting

Raffaello Sanzio, known as Raphael (1483-1520)
Portrait of Baldassare Castiglione, 1514-1515
Oil on canvas, 82 × 67 cm
☞ Denon wing, 1rst floor, room 5

Raphael painted many portraits. On this one, he portrayed Castiglione, a humanist personality from Mantua, author of the *Book of the Courtier*, remarkably successful in the 16th century. The painter pictures him as the perfect gentleman as he defines it in his textbook, namely soberly and richly dressed, imbued with a look with great acuteness.

Tiziano Vecellio, known as Titian (1488/1490-1576)
Man with a Glove, ca. 1520-1523
Oil on canvas, 100 × 89 cm
☞ Denon wing, 1rst floor, room 6

His reputation as a portraitist to the papal, royal and imperial courts (including Charles Quint's) allowed Titian to be treated as royal blood. The undisputed master of Venetian painting, he offers here a greatly naturalistic portrait, balancing between nonchalance and severity, with perfectly controlled contrasts of dark and light notes.

**Tiziano Vecellio,
known as Titian
(1488/1490-1576)**
The Country Concert,
ca. 1510
Oil on canvas, 105 × 137 cm
☛ Denon wing, 1rst floor,
room 6

There is a consensus to attribute this work to the Titian,
although its topic supposedly comes from Giorgione. Its
interpretation remains enigmatic. It could be an allegory
of poetry: naked women emanate from the imagination
of two men. Famous and often copied, it inspired Manet
for the equally famous 1863 *Luncheon on the Grass*.

**Paolo Caliari, known
as Veronese (1528-1588)**
The Wedding Feast at Cana,
1562-1563
Toile, 677 × 994 cm
☛ Denon wing, 1rst floor, room 6

The topic of this monumental
painting, commissioned
by the Benedictines of San
Giorgio Maggiore for their
refectory, provides Veronese
with an iconographic
pretext reinterpreted with
a great imagination. The
miraculous event of the
transformation of water
into wine inspires a banquet
scene comparable to a
sumptuous Venetian festival,
set up in the framework of
an architectural perspective
worthy of a 16th century
theater house. Mary and
Jesus stand at the center,
surrounded by a swarm of
characters - one hundred
and thirty - not paying them
any attention, except for
the disciples. A tribute to
Venetian opulence, the decor,
composed symmetrically,
shows marble - a material
that had gradually taken
the place of wood in the
building of the city -
glassware (through the arts
the table), and clothes that
give the canvas, with their
embroidery, shimmering
colors. The musicians in
the foreground supposedly
portray Venetian masters:
Titian, Tintoretto, Bassano
and Veronese himself,
dressed in white.

**Michelangelo Merisi,
known as Caravaggio
(1571-1610)**
The Fortune-Teller, ca. 1594
Oil on canvas, 99 × 131 cm
☛ Denon wing, 1rst floor,
room 8

With this secular theme – a gypsy steals a ring on the
pretext of reading the lines of the hands of her victim –
Caravaggio offers an innovative pictorial language that
was widely emulated. Attached to the representation
of reality and the working classes, the great master of
chiaroscuro demonstrates here a mannerist elegance
combined to a meticulous realist style.

**Michelangelo
Merisi, known
as Caravaggio
(1571-1610)**
*The Death of the
Virgin,* 1605-1606
Oil on canvas,
369 × 245 cm
☛ Denon wing,
1rst floor, room 8

Caravaggio used to ask models met
by chance on the street to pose for his
paintings. That is why this representation of
the Virgin, giving up the ghost, surrounded
by characters prey to overwhelming
emotions, seems so "human". The priests
of the church of Santa Maria della Scala, to
whom the picture was destined, refused it,
shocked by its naturalism.

Italian Painting

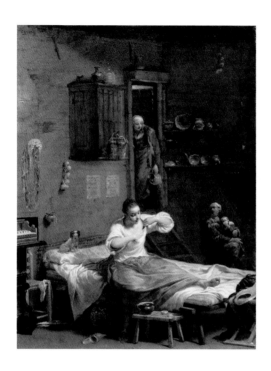

Giuseppe Maria Crespi
(1665-1747)
Searching for Fleas, ca. 1720-1730
Oil on canvas, 55 × 41 cm
☞ Denon wing, 1rst floor, room 26

This work is supposedly part
of a series about the life of a
female opera singer of low
extraction. A keen observer
of Dutch genre painting, the
Bolognese artist delivers a
pungent evocation, which plays
out as a sort of "treasure hunt",
making the onlooker search for
marks of wealth – breed dog,
slippers, perhaps an allusion
to the generosity of a lover –
scattered in a modest setting.

Giandomenico Tiepolo
(1727-1804)
Carnival Scene,
ca. 1754-1755
Oil on canvas, 80 × 110 cm
☛ Denon wing, 1rst floor,
room 26

A devoted aide to his father Giambattista, who established himself as the greatest designer of his time, and to whom this painting was long attributed, Giandomenico Tiepolo was nevertheless able to achieve true personal work, including representations of the carnival in the Venice of his time, then in strong political and economic decline.

Francesco Guardi
(1712-1793)
The Doge of Venice at Carnival Thursday on the Piazzetta,
1766-1770
Oil on canvas, 67 × 100 cm
☛ Denon wing,
1rst floor, room 26

Guardi, the last great representative of Venetian painting, became, just like Canaletto, illustrious thanks to a booming genre of the 18th century, *Veduta*, the painting of the architectural splendors of the city for tourists. This painting belongs to a series depicting the ceremonies held for the election of Doge Alvise IV Mocenigo.

S.POLO
NIA.

Francisco de Zurbarán (1598-1664)
St. Apollonia, ca. 1636
Oil on canvas, 116 × 66 cm
☛ Denon wing, 1rst floor, room 26

Regarded in the seventeenth century as the "Spanish Caravaggio", Zurbarán carried out a brilliant career in Seville and Madrid, where his sense of the human figure, the flexibility of his line, and his chromatic energy were very much appreciated. The Saint, who appears rosy-cheeked and dressed in shimmering cloths, is Apolline, a second century martyr: because she was a Christian, legend has it that they broke her jaw and shattered her teeth. She stares frontally at the viewer, holding the attributes of her ordeal. The elegance and realism of details permeate this work with a secular mind.

Domenikos Theotokopoulos, known as El Greco (1541-1614)
Christ on the Cross adored by two donors, 1576-1579
Oil on canvas,
260 × 171 cm
☛ Denon wing, 1rst floor, room 26

This crucifixion, painted in Toledo, reflects the uniqueness of El Greco, an artist originally from Crete, who spent most of his career in Spain after staying in Venice and Rome, where he assimilated the lessons of the late mannerism, especially Tintoretto's. The sponsors, unidentified, are at the feet of the dying Jesus, while the background is occupied by a mass of thick and dark clouds.

Spanish Painting

Jusepe de Ribera (1591-1652)
The Clubfoot, 1642
Oil on canvas, 164 × 93 cm
☛ Denon wing, 1rst floor, room 26

The artist, who spent most of his career in Naples in the service of the Spanish viceroys, had a strong influence on his fellow artists of the Spanish Golden Age with his popular scenes. Here, he painted with great realism the deformities of the young cripple who holds in his hand the act authorizing him to be a beggar, written in Latin: "Give me alms for the love of God."

Bartolomé Esteban Murillo (1618-1682)
The Young Beggar, ca. 1650
Oil on canvas, 134 × 110 cm
☛ Denon wing, 1rst floor, room 26

Animated by strong contrasts between darkness and natural daylight, this genre scene shows a street child stripping. At his feet, lay shrimp peels, the remains of a frugal meal. This type of sentimental imaging enjoyed great iconographic fortune. The Sevillian artist detaches himself from Caravaggio's tenebrism through a brightened palette.

**Francisco de Goya y
Lucientes (1746-1828)**
*Portrait of the Condesa
del Carpio*, known as
*The Marquesa de la
Solana*, ca. 1793-1794
Oil on canvas, 181 × 122 cm
☛ Sully wing, 2nd floor,
room A

Goya painted this portrait of Maria Rita
Barrenechea, wife of Count del Carpio, during
the second part of his career, in which he broke free
of his search for official positions to express himself
more freely. He renewed the conception of the art
of portrait as his master Velázquez saw it, under
the influence of the great contemporary English
portraitists such as Gainsborough and Reynolds.
The model's stature suggests his admiration
for this well-read woman, while the scarred face
reflects his compassion for her: it is upon learning
of her inevitable and upcoming death that she
commissioned this portrait of herself for her
daughter.

Northern Painting

Jan Van Eyck
(ca. 1390/1400-1441)
*The Virgin at the home of
Chancellor Rolin*, ca. 1435
Oil on wood, 66 × 62 cm
☛ Richelieu wing, 2nd floor,
room 5

Van Eyck is credited for the discovery of oil painting
– although he perfected it more than he invented it –
which allowed a very accurate rendering. The sponsor
of this work, Nicolas Rolin, chancellor of Burgundy,
is portrayed in the same proportions as the Virgin
and Child to whom he prays. Considered a fabulous
illusionist, the artist depicts very realistically, in the
background, an imaginary landscape.

**Rogier Van der Weyden
(1399/1400-1464)
(studio)**
The Annunciation, ca. 1435
Oil on wood, 86 × 93 cm

The painter, born in Tournai, is, along with Van Eyck,
the founder of the great Flemish tradition of the
15th century. It is in a comfortable and richly decorated
contemporary interior that he decided to set his
Annunciation, probably executed after his formulas by
his studio shortly after he settled in Brussels circa 1435.

Hieronymus Bosch (ca. 1450-1516)
The Ship of Fools, ca. 1490-1500
Oil on wood, 58 × 32 cm
☞ Richelieu wing, 2nd floor, room 6

Highly regarded during the
16th century, the work of Bosch,
saturated with symbols, must be seen
in the context of the spiritual crisis
of the era, marked by the publication
of *In Praise of Folly* by Erasmus.
This ship adrift denounces, through
nightmarish weather conditions, the
dissolution of a clergy lost in excesses
and the disorientation of Christians.

**Pieter Bruegel the Elder
(ca. 1525-1569)**
The Beggars, 1568
Oil on wood, 18 × 21 cm
☞ Richelieu wing, 2nd floor, room 12

A humanist artist examining with a
sarcastic eye the morals of his time,
Bruegel portrays here a group of
legless cripples. The interpretation
of this scene is enigmatic: is it a
carnivalesque parody, each character
embodying a social group, or an
evocation of the "revolt of beggars",
the Dutch uprising against the
Spanish rule?

**Quentin Metsys
(1465/1566-1530)**
*The Moneylender
and his wife*, 1514
Oil on wood, 70 × 67 cm
☛ Richelieu wing, 2nd floor,
room 9

This painting, executed in the rich city of Antwerp,
where the artist pursued a brilliant career after training
in Leuven, marks the beginning of the Dutch genre
painting. The eyes of the woman who turns away from
her prayer book to scrutinize the money handled by her
husband suggests a moralizing intent. Metsys inserted
in the mirror in the foreground, a fascinating tiny self-
portrait.

Northern Painting

Peter Paul Rubens (1577-1640)
Helena Fourment with a carriage, ca. 1639
Oil on wood, 195 × 132 cm
☛ Richelieu wing, 2nd floor, room 21

The Antwerp-born artist, highly regarded throughout Europe, was also a shrewd businessman, leading a busy workshop. The opulence visible in this portrait of his second wife, dressed Spanish-style in black clothes, with his son Frans, is a testament to the painter's success, representative of the prestigious Flemish Baroque.

Antoon Van Dyck (1599-1641)
Charles I, King of England, at the hunt, ca. 1635-1638
Oil on canvas, 266 × 207 cm
☛ Richelieu wing, 2nd floor, room 24

A precocious artist who soon imposed himself as Rubens' best assistant in Antwerp, Van Dyck soon emancipated from his master, to be coveted by the greatest European courts. He enjoyed a brilliant career in England, where he portrayed King Charles I, in an innovative posture, dismounting during a hunting party.

**Peter Paul Rubens
(1577-1640)**
*The Landing at Marseilles
on 3rd November 1600,*
1622-1625

Oil on canvas, 394 × 295 cm

☞ Richelieu wing, 2nd floor,
room 18

This painting is part of a cycle of twenty-four
commissioned by Marie de Medici, widow of
Henri IV, illustrating the life of the regent. This work
of glorification mixes real events – here, the arrival in
France of the queen after her marriage in Florence –
and supernatural creatures (Nereids and sea gods)
to give them a mythical dimension.

Northern Painting

**Frans Hals
(1581/1585-1666)**
The Gypsy Girl,
ca. 1628-1630
Oil on canvas, 58 × 52 cm
☞ Richelieu wing,
2nd floor, room 28

Hals, who became famous only late in life, spent his entire career in Haarlem. He mostly asserts himself as a talented portraitist, able to capture the beauty of faces, such as this intriguing woman and her sidelong glance. His touch, felt in the rendering of complexions and pleated sleeves, infuses an expression of intense life into the painting.

**Jacob Jordaens
(1593-1678)**
The King drinks,
ca. 1638-1640
Oil on canvas, 152 × 204 cm
☛ Richelieu wing, 2nd floor,
room 19

To Jordaens, the celebration of the Epiphany is the opportunity to portray scenes of earthy, or even Dionysian, popular rejoicing. A major representative of the Flemish Baroque style, the artist operates a typically carnivalesque flipping of social values with this complex composition, marked by the influence of Rubens and Italian painting.

Northern Painting

Rembrandt Harmensz. van Rijn, known as Rembrandt (1606-1669)
Portrait of the Artist at his Easel, 1660
Oil on canvas, 111 × 90 cm
☞ Richelieu wing, 2nd floor, room 31

With a career marked by successes, bankruptcy, and a tumultuous love life, Rembrandt documented, through his numerous self-portraits, his moral and physical development. Here he portrays himself, aged fifty-four, without complacency, unshaven and in a gown. Facing his easel, he seems to assert his status as a modest craftsman in a chiaroscuro characteristic of his style.

Rembrandt Harmensz. Van Rijn, known as Rembrandt (1606-1669)
The Flayed Ox, 1655
Oil on wood, 94 × 69 cm
☞ Richelieu wing, 2nd floor, room 31

This ox carcass, at first glance the opposite of any quest for beauty, delivers a picture of a rare dramatic intensity. Exploring the material effects of painting and the expressive power of contrasts, Rembrandt ultimately signs here a *Vanitas,* symbol of the futility of life.

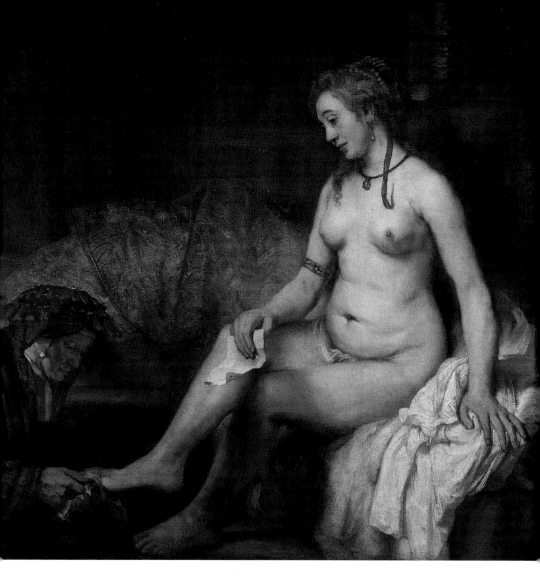

**Rembrandt Harmensz.
van Rijn, known as
Rembrandt (1606-1669)**
Bathsheba Bathing,
1654
Oil on canvas, 142 × 142 cm
☞ Richelieu wing, 2nd floor,
room 31

King David, who desired Bathsheba after seeing her
bathing, undertook, in the absence of her husband,
to seduce her. Here, she is meditating over his letter
by which he invites her to join him. This episode
of the Sacred History is, for Rembrandt, a pretext
for a naturalist nude for which he exploited the features
of his last partner in life, Hendrickje Stoffels.

Northern Painting

Johannes Vermeer
(1632-1675)
The Lacemaker,
ca. 1670-1671
Oil on canvas, 24 × 21 cm
☞ Richelieu wing, 2nd floor,
room 38

It is possible that, in order to achieve this small, tightly framed and soberly colored work, Vermeer made use of the *camera obscura*, which can capture an image in an enclosed structure to trace it. This technique allows to focus the attention on the female figure, herself absorbed by her meticulous task.

Johannes Vermeer
(1632-1675)
The Astronomer, 1668
Oil on canvas, 51 × 45 cm
☛ Richelieu wing, 2nd floor, room 38

Stretching over twenty years, the production of the master from Delft is thin. Barely over thirty paintings are attributed to him, all marked by a virtuoso technique, based on a finite and extremely subtle brightness. Among a Dutch setting, an astronomer puts his hand on a celestial globe, symbol of knowledge and the quest for the afterlife.

Pieter De Hooch (1629-1684)
Young Woman Drinking, 1658

Oil on canvas, 69 × 60 cm

☛ Richelieu wing, 2nd floor, room 38

Although Pieter De Hooch follows the intimate genre painting, his originality lies in the construction of space. This conversation scene is complexified by the empty chair in the foreground, the *mise en abyme* of images (including *Christ and the adulteress* on the right) and the perspectivist treatment drawing the eye towards the background.

Jan Davidz. de Heem (1606-1683)
A Table of Desserts, 1640

Oil on canvas, 149 × 203 cm

☛ Richelieu wing, 2nd floor, room 38

A masterpiece of the artist's Antwerp period, which played a major role in the development of the still life in Flanders and Holland, this painting belongs to the *repas servis* ("served meals") genre. Purchased by Louis XIV and often copied – especially by Matisse in the 20th century – this work operates a brilliant synthesis between Dutch accuracy and Flemish Baroque.

Samuel Van Hoogstraten (1627-1678)
View of an Interior,
or *The Slippers*, 1658
Oil on canvas, 103 × 70 cm
☞ Sully wing, 2nd floor, room B

Hoogstraten's tour de force is to be able to tell a moralizing story "between the lines", without having to use any characters, only by the ordering of objects in space. The slippers, enhanced by a ray of light, suggest the abandonment of the home by a woman to meet a lover. In the background, hangs *The Paternal Admonition*, by Ter Borch, denouncing venal love.

Albrecht Dürer (1471-1528)
Portrait of the Artist holding a Thistle,
1493
Oil on parchment mounted on canvas,
56 × 44 cm
☞ Richelieu wing, 2nd floor, room 8

This very first self-portrait by Dürer
was perhaps made for his fiancée.
A precocious genius schooled in
Nuremberg, he embellishes it with
a sentence written above his head,
sounding like a predestination: "My
business is moving as planned in
high places." Hence the ambiguity
of the branch of holly he is holding:
it may symbolize Christ's crown
of thorns – the artist assimilating
his trade to a divine mission – or,
according to the German tradition,
a promise of fidelity to his beloved.

**Hans Holbein, the Younger
(1497/1498-1543)**
Nikolas Kratzer, 1528
Oil on wood, 83 × 67 cm
☞ Richelieu wing, 2nd floor, room B

Coming from a family of artists,
impregnated with the humanist
culture (he was close to Erasmus)
and the lessons of the Italian
Renaissance, Holbein traveled
extensively before settling in the
court of England. This is where he
portrayed the astronomer of King
Henry VIII, *Nicolas Kratzer,* busy
building a sundial.

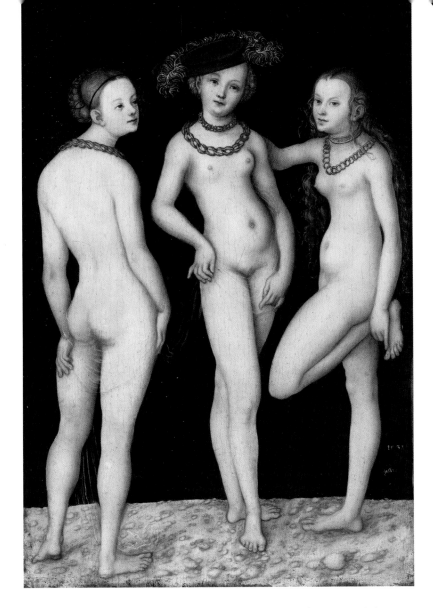

**Lucas Cranach the Elder
(1472-1553)**
The Three Graces, 1531
Oil on wood, 37 × 27 cm
☛ Richelieu wing, 2nd floor,
room 8

Court painter for the Electors of Saxony and close to
the humanist circles of the Reformation, Cranach set
himself as the master of a renewed eroticism, with
elongated nudes characterized by mannerist attitudes.
In this painting, showing three mythical women
– Euphrosyne, Aglaia and Thalia – joined by a veil,
he is able to illustrate his feminine canon from three
different angles, front, back and three-quarters.

German Painting

Caspar David Friedrich
(1774-1840)
The Tree of Crows, ca. 1822
Oil on canvas, 59 × 74 cm
☞ Richelieu wing, 2nd floor,
room E

A solitary artist, little known during his lifetime, Friedrich embodies today the essence of German romanticism, inhabited by the sense of the sacred and the taste for a sublime nature. Influenced by the theories of Goethe and Schelling, the artist evokes here a Hun tomb, remembrance of the pagan world, while, in the distance, looms Arkona on the Rügen Island, a symbolic place for the move toward Christianity.

Christen Schjellerup Købke
(1810-1848)
Portrait of Adolphine Købke, 1832
Oil on canvas, 42 × 35 cm
☛ Richelieu wing, 2nd floor, room D

Danish painting knew,
during the first half of the
19th century, a blooming,
thanks to landscape and
portrait painters of great talent,
able to render the cold clarity
of northern lights, which, in
this painting, enlighten the
boyish and sullen face of the
painter's sister, who executed
this portrait while he was at
the Academy of Copenhagen.

Carl Christian Constantin Hansen
(1804-1880)
Young Boys playing dice in front of the
Christiansburg Castle in Copenhagen, 1834
Oil on canvas, 60 × 51 cm
☛ Richelieu wing, 2nd floor, room D

Although the Christiansburg Palace in
Copenhagen provides the framework
for this genre scene, most of the work
lies in the freshness of these children
playing in the sun, rendered with a great
chromatic refinement. Hansen is one
of the major figures of the golden age
of Danish painting, heir to a brand of
classicism full of zest and excitement.

English Painting

**Thomas Gainsborough
(1727-1788)**
Conversation in a park,
ca. 1746-1747
Oil on canvas, 73 × 68 cm
☞ Denon wing, 1rst floor,
room 32

Gainsborough is certainly one of the greatest British painters of the 18th century, able to excel in a light register, flirting with the rococo, but also to give his models depth and sophistication. In this conversation scene that breaks with the conventions of the classic portrait, the painter paints himself with his wife. This work is characterized by a fluid facture and a science of details deriving from the observation of Flemish portraits.

**Joshua Reynolds
(1723-1792)**
Master Hare, ca. 1788-1789

Oil on canvas, 77 × 63 cm

☞ Denon wing, 1rst floor, room 32

Regarded as the leader of the English School, a major theorist in the history of art, and the first chairman of the Royal Academy, Reynolds was attached to the notion of "grand style". He nevertheless subverts here the tradition of portrait painting with this child in his muslin clothes, pointing out an object set out of frame arousing his curiosity. This famous portrait is a perfect example if an intimate and sensitive vein dealing with the theme of childhood.

English Painting

John Constable
(1776-1837)
Weymouth Bay with
approaching storm,
England, ca. 1819
Oil on canvas, 88 × 112 cm
☞ Denon wing, 1rst floor,
room 32

With Constable, a great admirer of the 17th century
Dutch landscape artists, as well as Lorrain and Poussin,
landscape painting takes on a new dimension, which
influenced the romantics, the Barbizon School and,
indirectly, the Impressionists: it is no longer the mere
translation of the external nature, but is an expression of
interiority, as is plainly visible on this view of the Dorset
coastline where rises a wall of clouds, the threatening
omens of a coming storm.

Joseph Mallord William Turner (1775-1851)
Landscape with a River and a Bay in the Distance, ca. 1835-1840
Oil on canvas, 93 × 123 cm
☛ Denon wing, 1rst floor, room 32

A precocious and self-taught artist, member of the Royal Academy, Turner wanted to compete with the art of the great masters, Lorrain, Poussin and Watteau. However, he increasingly devoted himself to rendering the effects of atmosphere and light. Despite some references – a stream leading to a lake, tree-lined banks, skies crowded with clouds – the forms of the landscape dissolve in the light, sliding from the optical imitation to the depiction of sensations.

Graphic Arts

For conservation reasons, the nearly 150,000 works of the Graphic Arts department are never on permanent display. Their fragility, particularly because of their sensitivity to light and moisture, requires their keeping in the reserves, except for their presentation during temporary exhibitions (never more than three consecutive months) or in the consulting rooms for reading. The Graphic Arts department derives, in part, from the Cabinet des Dessins, a remnant of the formal Royal collection, mostly constituted with the purchase, by Louis XIV, of banker Eberhardt Jabach's 5,562 drawings, but also of Charles Le Brun's and Nicolas Mignard's studio drawings; for another part, it is an emanation of the Louvre's Chalcographie, founded in 1797, to deal with copper engraving; and finally from the Edmond de Rothschild Collection, mostly made up of woodblock prints.

The graphic arts cover a wide range of techniques – drawings, miniatures, prints, pastels – and various schools throughout the centuries. The Louvre's collections are particularly well endowed in the field of French schools and Italian Renaissance and hold major works, including Leonardo da Vinci's, notably his extraordinary *Study of folds for a kneeling figure*. The department can measure the importance of drawing, in modern times, as an essential matrix for creating formal study tools before the final achievements (pictorial or architectural) are completed, and with the engraving, a vector for the dissemination of images. The graphics arts are not exempt of works with rich and abundant colors, such as the large pastel portrait of the Marquise de Pompadour by Quentin de La Tour, as well as inks and watercolors (landscapes by Constable and Delacroix) of the 19th century.

Graphic Arts

**Jean Fouquet
(ca. 1415/1420-1477/1481)**
*Saint Marguerite watching
her sheep*, ca. 1470-1475
Illumination on parchment
with gold highlights, 9.1 × 11.9 cm

Fouquet contributed to the revival of the 15th century illumination, through shimmering colors, the effects of perspective and a never seen before naturalism. *The Book of Hours* of Etienne Chevalier (whose pages are now dispersed) illustrates this scene from the Golden Legend: a Roman prefect falls in love with Marguerite, a Christian shepherdess spinning her distaff, ignoring her future torturer.

Albrecht Dürer (1471-1528)
The Arco Valley, 1495
Watercolor and gouache with black ink retakes
on parchment, 22.3 × 22.2 cm

This landscape is the result of an observation from nature by Dürer while traveling through Europe. In 1495, after a stay in Italy, he returned to Nuremberg and captured, near Lake Garda, the Arco citadel set upon a high rock. Tones of blue, green and gray confer a poetic touch in this highly accurate topographic study.

Leonardo di ser Piero da Vinci, aka Leonardo da Vinci (1452-1519)
Study of folds for a kneeling figure, late 15th- early 16th century
Grey tempera with white highlights on grey canvas, 28.1 × 20.7 cm

Leonardo treated, in theoretical as well as technical terms, the art of depicting draping and folds, an achievement regarded as fundamental during the Renaissance. This brush study on a linen canvas pictures folded legs, covered by a cloth falling heavily to the ground, seemingly initiating a slight twisting motion. It is commonly associated with the sketch of the *Virgin of the Annunciation*, preserved in the Uffizi in Florence.

Jean Siméon Chardin
(1699-1779)
Self-Portrait with Spectacles, 1771
Pastel on grey-blue paper, 45.9 × 37.5 cm

Not just a self-portrait of the artist at work, this pastel is a tribute to a fragile and subtle technique, of creating patterns with a powder effect, a low color saturation and a clarity full of freshness. In the last ten years of his life, Chardin also used it for health reasons, the solvent fumes of paint attacking his eyes.

Charles Le Brun (1619-1690)
Relationship of the human figure
with that of the Tawny Owl, ca. 1668
Black ink, gouache and black chalk
on white paper, 23.1 × 32 cm

First painter to King Louis XIV, Charles Le Brun tried to hierarchize the arts and to codify their rules. He suggested including through a series of plates, an illustration of his theories on human physiognomy and its relationship with animals, deeply imbued with the belief in an equivalence between physical and moral character traits.

Maurice Quentin Delatour, known as Quentin de La Tour (1704-1788)
Full-Length Portrait of the Marquise de Pompadour, 1755
Pastel on gray-blue paper with gouache highlights, the face is cut out and mounted on the paper, 177.5 × 130 cm

Quentin de La Tour, the master of pastel *par excellence* in the 18th century, gave the genre its masterpiece with this official portrait of the Marquise de Pompadour, depicted as the protector of arts and letters. Louis XV's favorite with is pictured here wearing a beautiful French-style dress and surrounded attributes symbolizing music, literature, astronomy, drawing and printmaking.

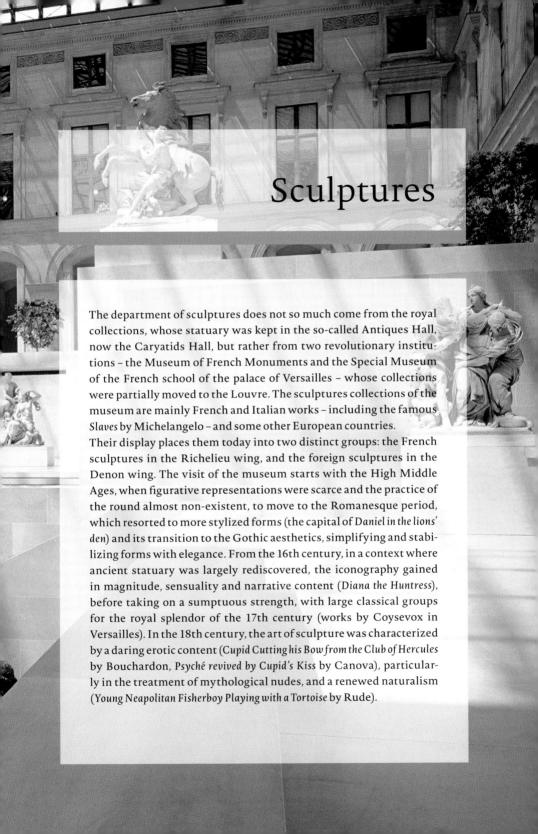

Sculptures

The department of sculptures does not so much come from the royal collections, whose statuary was kept in the so-called Antiques Hall, now the Caryatids Hall, but rather from two revolutionary institutions – the Museum of French Monuments and the Special Museum of the French school of the palace of Versailles – whose collections were partially moved to the Louvre. The sculptures collections of the museum are mainly French and Italian works – including the famous *Slaves* by Michelangelo – and some other European countries.

Their display places them today into two distinct groups: the French sculptures in the Richelieu wing, and the foreign sculptures in the Denon wing. The visit of the museum starts with the High Middle Ages, when figurative representations were scarce and the practice of the round almost non-existent, to move to the Romanesque period, which resorted to more stylized forms (the capital of *Daniel in the lions' den*) and its transition to the Gothic aesthetics, simplifying and stabilizing forms with elegance. From the 16th century, in a context where ancient statuary was largely rediscovered, the iconography gained in magnitude, sensuality and narrative content (*Diana the Huntress*), before taking on a sumptuous strength, with large classical groups for the royal splendor of the 17th century (works by Coysevox in Versailles). In the 18th century, the art of sculpture was characterized by a daring erotic content (*Cupid Cutting his Bow from the Club of Hercules* by Bouchardon, *Psyché revived by Cupid's Kiss* by Canova), particularly in the treatment of mythological nudes, and a renewed naturalism (*Young Neapolitan Fisherboy Playing with a Tortoise* by Rude).

Sculptures

Daniel in the lion's den
Paris, 6th and late 11th centuries
Marble, 49 × 53 × 51 cm
☞ Richelieu wing, ground floor, room 1

Used to transfer the load of
a column, a capital is also an
ornament. This one, from the
Sainte-Geneviève church in
Paris, evokes a scene from the
Old Testament in a style typical
of Romanesque architecture,
stripped, even abrupt: Daniel is
about to be devoured by lions.
His face is confident, a sign of
unshakable faith in God.

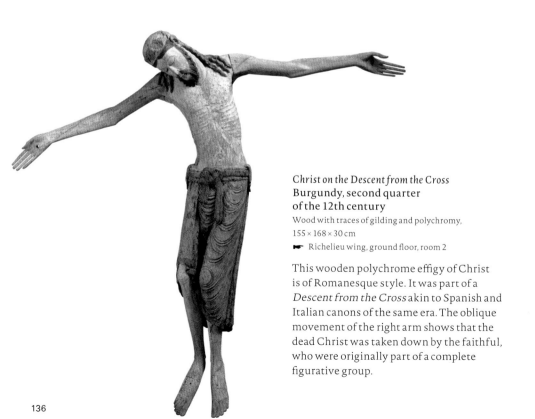

Christ on the Descent from the Cross
**Burgundy, second quarter
of the 12th century**
Wood with traces of gilding and polychromy,
155 × 168 × 30 cm
☞ Richelieu wing, ground floor, room 2

This wooden polychrome effigy of Christ
is of Romanesque style. It was part of a
Descent from the Cross akin to Spanish and
Italian canons of the same era. The oblique
movement of the right arm shows that the
dead Christ was taken down by the faithful,
who were originally part of a complete
figurative group.

Gregor Erhart
(ca. 1460-1540)
St. Mary Magdalene,
early 16th century
Lime tree wood, original
polychromy, 177 × 44 × 43 cm
☞ Denon wing, lower
ground floor, room C

This human-sized masterpiece combines two
registers with subtlety, that of holiness and of a
renowned sense of sensuality. Retired to a cave
in the Massif de la Sainte-Baume in Provence,
to atone for her sins, wearing her hair as only
clothing, Mary Magdalene inspires the German
sculptor a truly modern nude, fully colored and
three-dimensional.

Sculptures

Germain Pilon (ca. 1528-1590)
Funerary Monument for the heart of Henri II:
Les Trois Grâces, ca. 1560-1566
Marble, 150 × 75.5 × 75.5 cm
☛ Richelieu wing, ground floor, room 15a

A collaborative effort between craftsmen of several trades, this sculpture owes its primary group to Germain Pilon, renowned for his royal tombs. The goddesses, back to back, form a rhythmic and elegant roundel, bearing on their heads a copper vessel concealing the heart of Henry II. The Latin epitaph begins with these words: "Here Queen Catherine, wishing to hide it in her own breast, put down the heart of her husband."

Fontainebleau School
Diana the Huntress, known as
Diane of Anet, mid-16th century
Marble, 211 × 258 × 134 cm
☛ Richelieu wing, ground floor, room 15b

This is the first large nude sculpture in French art, from the castle of Diane de Poitiers, mistress of Henri II, in Anet. It figures the goddess of the hunt, accompanied by her dogs and hugging a deer, symbol of the king. Diane's posture is reminiscent of the famous high relief *The Nymph of Fontainebleau* by Benvenuto Cellini. Despite various names mentioned – Jean Goujon, Germain Pilon, Pierre Bontemps or Ponce Jacquiot – this pinnacle of elegant mannerism and sensuality remains unattributed.

**Michelangelo Buonarroti,
known as Michel-Ange (1475-1564)**
Slave, also called *The Dying Slave*,
1513-1515 (unfinished)
Marbre, 227.7 × 72.4 × 53.5 cm
☛ Denon wing, ground floor, room 4

Michelangelo, who claimed
throughout his career his preference
for sculpture, crafted the *Dying Slave*
to adorn the tomb of Pope Julius II,
which was never completed. This
body, close the canons of Antiquity,
may symbolize an incarnation of the
provinces subdued by the warrior
pope, or the soul imprisoned by human
passions.

Sculptures

Pierre Puget (ca. 1620-1694)
Milo of Croton, 1670-1682
Marble, 270 × 140 × 98 cm
☛ Richelieu wing, lower ground
floor, Puget courtyard

As part of a large order
by Louis XIV to ornate
the gardens of Versailles,
Puget picked a rarely
addressed topic. This
delivered a dramatic piece
depicting Milo of Croton,
a famed pugilist of ancient
Greece, ultimately defeated
by his own pride. The aging
athlete finds himself prisoner
of an oak he wanted to take
down with his bare hands,
and a wild beast seizes the
opportunity to strike him.

Antoine Coysevox (1640-1720)
Mercury Riding Pegasus, 1699-1702
Marble, 315 × 291 × 128 cm
☛ Richelieu wing, lower ground floor,
Marly courtyard

A prominent protagonist of the
French classicism and "number
one" sculptor of Louis XIV's court,
Coysevox achieved this allegory
of Fame, which trumpets the
glory of the monarch all through
the park of the Marly castle. His
unique feat in this work is the
crafting without any connection
of the various forms – some very
fine (the trumpet) – in regard
to the monumental dimensions
of this group.

Guillaume I Coustou (1677-1746)
Horse Restrained by a Groom, known as *Horse of Marly,* 1739-1745

Marble, 340 × 284 × 127 cm

☞ Richelieu wing, lower ground floor, Marly courtyard

Coustou's Horses are directly inspired by those of his uncle Coysevox, since Louis XV ordered them to fill the gap left in Park of Marly after their transfer to the Tuileries. The nephew competed with his elder by carving, as he had, the animals from a monolithic block of marble, but also by sacrificing any allegorical reference for an abrupt depiction of nature.

Sculptures

Edme Bouchardon (1698-1762)
Cupid Cutting His Bow from the Club of Hercules, 1739-1750
Marble, 173 × 75 × 75 cm
☛ Richelieu wing, ground floor, room 23

This work, which occupied Bouchardon for a very long time, is representative of the naturalistic endeavors of the 18th century. While the mythological topic suggests the artist's passion for Antique sculpture, the body is portrayed according to the anatomical shape of an adolescent, a lewdness that did not fail to offend the artist's contemporaries.

Augustin Pajou (1730-1809)
Psyche Abandoned, 1790
Marble, 177 × 86 × 86 cm
☛ Richelieu wing, ground floor, room 27

This commission from the King's Buildings, as a counterpart to Bouchardon's *Cupid*, was supposed to remain in place for five days only at the 1785 Salon. Pajou, while seeking to reconcile ancient tradition and naturalist truth, was probably too bold by setting Psyche in a full nude. The scandal, however, contributed to the sculpture's reputation.

**Antonio Canova
(1757-1822)**
*Psyche Revived by Cupid's
Kiss*, 1793
Marble, 155 × 168 × 101 cm
☞ Denon wing, ground floor,
room 4

The Venetian artist triumphed throughout Europe as
the master of neoclassical sculpture, able to combine
an exemplary purity of lines with a sensuality imbued
with life. This work focuses on a complex balance of the
two mythological figures: Cupid lands near Psyche who,
waking, bends up to embrace the winged god, thanks to
whom she becomes immortal.

Sculptures

François Rude (1784-1855)
Young Neapolitan Fisherboy Playing with a Tortoise, 1831-1833
Marble, 82 × 88 × 48 cm
☞ Richelieu wing, ground floor, room 33

The display of this work at the 1833 Salon marked a break in the history of art. Rude assume the fact that an anecdotic genre scene, devoid of any mythological reference or edification purpose, can be carved from marble, a precious and noble material. Despite some controversy, this work earned him success and official honors.

Jean-Jacques Pradier, known as James Pradier (1790-1852)
Satyr and Bacchante, 1834
Marble, 128 × 112 × 78 cm
☞ Richelieu wing, ground floor, room 32

Pradier's style is still imbued with neoclassical elegance, but the sculptor confers it more shady and feverish accents, in the wake of romanticism. His career was hampered by the critiques of his contemporaries, especially at the sight of this faun assaulting a Bacchante with a brutal and carnal sensuality.

**Antoine Louis Barye
(1795-1875)**
Lion and serpent, 1832-1835
Bronze, 135 × 178 × 96 cm

Animal art, although centuries old, enjoyed a great development with Barye. The artist attended the menagerie of the Jardin des Plantes, where he studied the faces and attitudes of various species. The majestic power of the roaring lion is a symbolic tribute to the authority of Louis-Philippe after his accession to power in 1830.

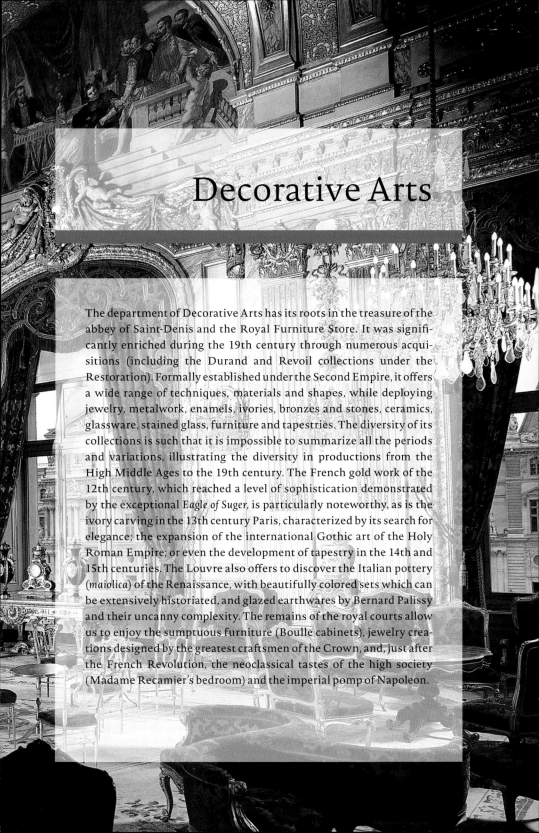

Decorative Arts

The department of Decorative Arts has its roots in the treasure of the abbey of Saint-Denis and the Royal Furniture Store. It was significantly enriched during the 19th century through numerous acquisitions (including the Durand and Revoil collections under the Restoration). Formally established under the Second Empire, it offers a wide range of techniques, materials and shapes, while deploying jewelry, metalwork, enamels, ivories, bronzes and stones, ceramics, glassware, stained glass, furniture and tapestries. The diversity of its collections is such that it is impossible to summarize all the periods and variations, illustrating the diversity in productions from the High Middle Ages to the 19th century. The French gold work of the 12th century, which reached a level of sophistication demonstrated by the exceptional *Eagle of Suger*, is particularly noteworthy, as is the ivory carving in the 13th century Paris, characterized by its search for elegance; the expansion of the international Gothic art of the Holy Roman Empire; or even the development of tapestry in the 14th and 15th centuries. The Louvre also offers to discover the Italian pottery (*maiolica*) of the Renaissance, with beautifully colored sets which can be extensively historiated, and glazed earthwares by Bernard Palissy and their uncanny complexity. The remains of the royal courts allow us to enjoy the sumptuous furniture (Boulle cabinets), jewelry creations designed by the greatest craftsmen of the Crown, and, just after the French Revolution, the neoclassical tastes of the high society (Madame Recamier's bedroom) and the imperial pomp of Napoleon.

Decorative Arts

The Emperor Triumphant, also called *Ivoire Barberini*, Constantinople, first half of the 6th century
Ivory, 34.2 × 26.8 × 2.8 cm
☞ Richelieu wing, 1rst floor, room 1

This almost complete leaflet of an imperial diptych exalts the triumph of a Byzantine emperor, probably Justinian, at the height of glory because of the peace he had just concluded with the Persians in 532. The central high-relief represents him lording over the conquered peoples, pictured in the lower part paying their tribute, and topped with a Christ in blessing.

Eagle-Shaped Vase, known as *Suger Eagle*, Saint-Denis abbey treasure, Roman or Egyptian antique vase, mount prior to 1147

Red porphyry, gilded silver, and niello, 43.1 × 27 cm
☛ Richelieu wing, 1rst floor, room 2

Abbot Suger commissioned for the abbey of Saint-Denis this antique porphyry vase to be remade in the shape of an eagle. The naturalism of the head and the stylization of the plumage come from a remarkable work of Ile-de-France goldsmiths. To Suger, adviser to Louis VI and Louis VII, the richness of religious art would contribute to enforce the relationship of the faithful to the Divine.

Equestrian Statuette of Charlemagne or Charles the Bald, **Metz Cathedral treasury, 9th century**
Bronze, formerly gilded, H. 23.5 cm
☛ Richelieu wing, 1rst floor, room 1

This equestrian statue – depicting Charlemagne or his grandson Charles the Bald – is directly inspired from the antique repertory: the rider has the appearance of a new Caesar with his world globe and his sword (missing). The proportions between the character and his mount do not coincide, the latter seemingly crafted at a later date.

13th century-16th century

Virgin and Child, Paris Sainte-Chapelle treasure,
third quarter of the 13th century
Ivory, formerly polychromic, 41 × 12.40 cm
☛ Richelieu wing, 1rst floor, room 3

During the 13th century, Paris became the capital of
ivory crafting. This slender Virgin and Child in the round,
perfectly proportioned and animated by a slight swaying,
is one of its most egregious florets. From the treasury
of the Sainte-Chapelle, it is a culmination of Gothic
aesthetics.

Scepter of Charles V, Saint-Denis abbey
treasure, prior to 1390
Gold, pearls, precious stones, glass, H. 60 cm
☛ Richelieu wing, 1rst floor, room 4

Appearing in the 14th century under the reign
of Charles V, the scepter intended to exalt
the royal power. It was held until the coming
of Charles X to the throne in 1825.
It is topped with a lily-shaped gold sheet and
the effigy of Charlemagne to underline the
commitment of the Valois line to the glorious
ancestry of the Carolingians.

Léonard Limosin (vers 1505-1575)
*Portrait of High Constable Anne
de Montmorency*, 1556

Painted enamel on copper, giltwood mount,
72 × 56 cm

☛ Richelieu wing, 1rst floor, room 21

The city of Limoges established itself
as a prominent center of the painted
enamel work during the 16th century,
under the leadership of the Limosin
family. The painted enamel technique
was initially devoted to the realization
of devotional paintings, portraits, and
decorative dishes. This effigy figures
Anne de Montmorency, an extremely
powerful personality close to kings
Francis I and Henry II, and a major
patron of the arts.

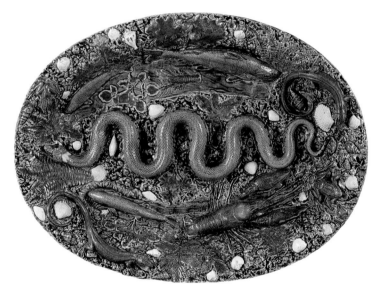

**Bernard Palissy
(1510?-1590)**
Dish with "rustic figulines",
ca. 1560

Glazed clay, lead glaze, 53 × 40 cm

☛ Richelieu wing, 1rst floor

Bernard Palissy was the greatest French ceramist of the
16th century. He devoted himself with a humanistic
curiosity to technical, scientific and aesthetic studies
to take the art of pottery to a pinnacle of sophistication
and whimsies. He is best known for his rustic *figulines*
with rich decors of figures in relief (fruits, plants,
animals, shells).

Decorative Arts

Aiguiere, 1rst century BC-1rst century AD, with 17th century additions by Pierre Delabarre, ca. 1630
Mounting, enameled gold, rubies, 27 × 16 × 10 cm
☞ Denon wing, 1rst floor, room 66

Louis XIV was very fond of hardstone vases. This aiguiere from his collection consists of an antique sardonyx vase decorated with an enameled gold mounting set with jewels. Its handle is dragon-shaped and the lid figures the head of Minerva. The technical virtuosity of Pierre Delabarre had a deep influence on the jewelry of the time.

Martin Carlin (ca. 1730-1785) and Charles-Nicolas Dodin (1734-1803)
Guéridon, Sèvres porcelain manufacture, 1774
Oak frame, amaranth veneer, soft porcelain, gilt bronze, mahogany, 81.7 × 80 cm
☞ Sully wing, 1rst floor

This *guéridon* table, a collaboration between the cabinetmaker Martin Carlin and porcelain painter Charles-Nicolas Dodin, was intended for the oval parlor of Madame du Barry's (last mistress of Louis XV) Louveciennes castle. The central plate shows the taste of the time for turqueries, while love scenes punctuate the perimeter.

**André-Charles Boulle
(1642-1732)**
Armoire (Wardrobe),
ca. 1700

Ebony veneer; marquetry
of brass, pewter, tortoiseshell
and horn; gilded bronze,
255 × 157 × 58 cm

☞ Sully wing, 1rst floor

While André-Charles Boulle was neither the inventor
nor the sole author of ebony furniture and precious
woods inlaid with copper, tin, tortoiseshell, ivory or
mother of pearl, decorated with gilt and chiseled bronze,
he gave them his name. Becoming one of the largest
suppliers to the Court in 1672, he crafted this one-body
wardrobe with two large doors decorated with flowers
inlays in the later years of Louis XIV's reign.

153

Decorative Arts

Martin Guillaume Biennais (1764-1843)
Tea set of Napoleon I and Marie-Louise, 1810
Gilt silver
☛ Richelieu wing, 1rst floor, room 70

The service was delivered by Biennais for the wedding of Napoleon and Marie-Louise in 1810, after the repudiation of Josephine de Beauharnais. Following a model by Charles Percier, it is very marked by a taste in antique shapes and motifs, with a very broad mythological repertoire, in accordance with a style dubbed "neoclassical."

Martin Guillaume Biennais (1764-1843)
"Charlemagne's" crown, 1804
Vermeil, cameos and intaglios, velvet and embroidered festoon
☛ Denon wing, 1rst floor, room 66

Napoleon commissioned from his appointed goldsmith Martin Guillaume Biennais this crown embellished with cameos from the head reliquary of St. Benedict in the abbey of Saint-Denis for his coronation on 2 December 1804 in Notre-Dame de Paris. This symbolic instrument of propaganda referred to the greatness of Charlemagne, last emperor to reign over France.

Jacob frères, from Louis Berthault (1770-1823)
Madame Récamier's Bedroom, ca. 1799
Mahogany, gilt and patinated bronze
☞ Richelieu wing, 1rst floor, room 69

The mansion of Madame Recamier was one of the most popular places in Paris, dictating the fashions of the time. Its very admired décor, by the architect Berthault, heralded the Empire style, as evidenced by this bed that already shows all the Empire classic features, namely a plain massiveness and antiquity inspiration in the ornamentation of bronze.

Arts of Africa, Asia, Oceania and the Americas

The collections of what is commonly called the *"arts premiers"*, or "Tribal arts", include, in the Louvre, one hundred and eight masterpieces from four main geographical areas: Africa, Asia, Oceania and the Americas. The rooms dedicated to them in the Pavillon des Sessions, opened in 2000 and designed by architect Jean-Michel Wilmotte, are a branch of the Musée du Quai Branly, which also manages the selection of the works displayed since most of them, originally kept in the Ethnology laboratory of the National Museum of Natural History or the National Museum of Arts of Africa and Oceania, actually belong to Branly. It is to the expert Jacques Kerchache that we owe the completion of this section, which establishes the recognition of the arts of Africa, Asia, Oceania and the Americas in the history of Western aesthetics.

As early as 1827, under the reign of Charles X, the Louvre Museum included a Marine and Ethnography department, then called the Dauphin's Museum, where the "exotic" artefacts brought back by the great explorers could be examined. However, in 1878, Jules Ferry ordered a distinction between "the history of manners and customs" and the "field of art." This decision has long relegated the worth of these items to their ethnographic interest. However, the 1200 square meters of the Pavillon des Sessions are not intended to provide a summary of the history of non-European productions, but to demonstrate their exemplarity and legitimize the exceptional artistic qualities of peoples too long ignored or even despised, although they make up 80% of mankind. Long after the "arts premiers" greatly influenced the avant-garde of the 20th century, their presence at the Louvre should encourage the renewal of the public eye on their beauty.

Arts of Africa, Asia, Oceania and the Americas

Female Figure
Mexico, Chupicuaro, 600-100 BC
Slipped terracotta, H. 31 cm
☛ Pavillon des Sessions, ground floor, room 7

This sculpture, over two thousand years old, has been found in the mountains of central Mexico. With generous volumes, it symbolizes the cycle of the seasons, as well as life and death. Its trapezoidal shape and black and cream patterns are surprisingly modern.

Male head
South-West Nigeria, Yoruba region, Ife culture, 12th-14th century
Terracotta, H. 15.5 cm
☛ Pavillon des Sessions, ground floor, room 2

A remnant of the civilization of Ife, regarded by the Yoruba people as the cradle of humanity, this modeled terracotta head portraying the servant of a deity mixes naturalism (with its streaks of scarification) and idealization.

Swan and white whale mask
Alaska, Kuskokwim river region,
Napaskiak village, Yup'ik (Inuit) culture,
early 20th century
Painted wood and feathers, H. 72 cm
☛ Pavillon des Sessions, ground floor, room 8

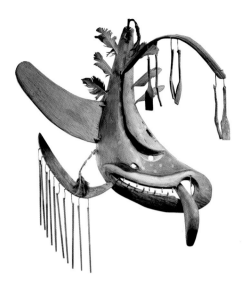

This mask, used by the Inuit for their ritual
dances, depicts a swan, an animal regarded as
an intercessor helping the hunt of white whales.
It belonged to surrealist writer André Breton,
who was probably very sensitive to its dreamlike
strange shapes.

Statue of ancestor (adu zatua) north of Nias Island, Indonesia, 19th century
Wood with red patina, H. 55.7 cm
☛ Pavillon des Sessions, ground floor, room 3

Statuettes used as recipients for the spirit of an ancestor, the
adu, were kept in homes to protect their denizens and, during
celebrations, used by priests to ensure the prosperity of the
community. The originality of this effigy lies in the contrast
between the posture of the man and the sophistication
of his traditional headdress.

Müyü ne bu: Magic stone used for buying castrated male pigs, Vanuatu, North of Ambryn Island, 18th-early 19th century
Volcanic tuff, H. 35.5 cm
☛ Pavillon des Sessions, ground floor, room 4

Stones imbued with magical properties, or *müyü ne bu*, are
still widespread in the Vanuatu archipelago. Characterized by
an exceptional formal audacity, with its curves and counter-
curves, this one is supposed to depict the powerful spirit
Lengnangoulong is supposed to make its owner richer in pigs.

Given their fragility, or because of a temporary displacement, a current display at the Louvre-Lens, or a loan for an exhibition, some of the works reproduced in this guide may not be visible in the museum exhibition rooms at the time of your visit.

Captions
Pages 8-9: Khorsabad courtyard with winged man-headed bulls; **pages 18-19:** Islamic arts departement hall, topped with the Visconti courtyard veil; **pages 26-27:** first Egyptian room of the Charles X museum; **pages 40-41:** Caryatids hall; **pages 52-53:** picture rail with, front, Jean Antoine Watteau's *Pierrot*, formerly known as *Le Gilles* (ca. 1718-1719); **pages 128-129:** 16th century Italian cartoons room; **pages 134-135:** Marly courtyard; **pages 146-147:** Napoléon III Apartments quoin Grand Salon; **pages 156-157:** hall of the Pavillon des Sessions.

Musée du Louvre
Henri Loyrette
President and Director
Hervé Barbaret
Managing Director
Claudia Ferrazzi
Deputy Managing Director
Juliette Armand
Cultural Production Manager
Violaine Bouvet-Lanselle
Head of Publishing Department

Éditions Artlys
Séverine Cuzin-Schulte
Director of Publications
Lucile Desmoulins
Publisher
Rémy Goavec
Translator
Catherine Enault
Graphic Designer
Pierre Kegels
Head of Production

Établissement P & J
Graphic Design

Fotimprim
Photogravure

Timedian
Printing

Printed February 28, 2013
in Villejust by Timedian
Legal Deposit: March 2013